"From Maestro to Magnate 1
and the fulfillment of a dream! This book provides a stirring testament to the reality of God's love for people and His desire to work through their lives. Author Sam Coryell takes his readers on a journey providing them with a poignant reminder of just how big God's plans are for each person."
 —John Lindell, Pastor, James River Assembly, Ozark MO

"It is often said that truth is better than fiction and that certainly is the case as you read *From Maestro to Magnate* by Sam Coryell. This warm autobiography reviews some of the joys and challenges of a very successful career."
 —Robert H. Spence, President, Evangel College

"Sam Coryell has a remarkable life story, and his willingness to share it and his business insights will undoubtedly benefit readers and students of success. Sam is a man of honesty, ingenuity, and faith, and is wholly committed to improving the lives of those around him. His life is a great example of how those traits can be combined to produce personal and professional triumphs."
 —Matt Blunt, former Governor of Missouri

"The passion and commitment of Samuel Coryell make his narrative both interesting and informative. The educational experiences for both Sam and his wife, Carol, are foundational—not only for university teaching careers but also for the transition which led to the development of an extremely successful real estate investment business (TLC Properties). The practical challenges of borrowing money and working with loaning institutions—of growing a business and making it work—will inspire and encourage every prospective entrepreneur."
 —Dr. Joe Nicholson, former chairman of the music
 department at Evangel University and Vice President of
 Global University of the Assemblies of God

To Shirley,
"Now may the LORD of peace
Himself give you peace at all
times and in every way. The LORD
be with you" (2Th. 3:16).

Blessings,

Sam

From Maestro to Magnate

An American Success Story

Dr. Sam Coryell

Gazelle
PRESS

Mobile, Alabama

From Maestro to Magnate
by Dr. Sam Coryell
Copyright ©2013 Samuel E. Coryell

Unless otherwise identified, Scripture is taken from *THE HOLY BIBLE: New International Version* ©1978 by the New York International Bible Society, used by permission of Zondervan Bible Publishers.

ISBN 978-1-58169-478-9
For Worldwide Distribution
Printed in the U.S.A.

Gazelle Press
P.O. Box 191540 • Mobile, AL 36619
800-367-8203

Contents

Introduction

Recently, I was reading the account in Mark about Jesus' healing of Peter's mother-in-law:

Simon's mother-in-law was in bed with a fever, and they told Jesus about her. So he went to her, took her hand and helped her up. The fever left her and she began to wait on them (Mk. 1:30–31).

As I reflected on this healing miracle, I realized that this woman was a senior citizen and perhaps looking forward to her golden years. Then, another realization hit me like a bolt of lightning. Although she may have felt she was on the "down" side of her useful ministry, Jesus took the time to give this woman the "touch" she needed to finish not only that day but her life's work as well. The Life-giver had visited her and she would never be the same again.

Her immediate response of service to Jesus and her other guests is what Jesus asks of all of His children. I could see that this encounter with the Son of God healed her not only for the short term but also for the "race" of life she still had ahead of her. The idea of "finishing strong" began to intrigue me.

Having had successful music careers in our early years, my wife, Carol, and I took up a the challenge of embarking on a second career in real estate during our later years. We could have coasted along in the field of music, but God presented us with a golden opportunity and we took it on with enthusiasm. Along the way, we have seen His hand on our lives and the lives of our entire family in our real estate endeavors.

Two careers along the way have given me a double appreciation for those who paved the way to make both of them possible. To accomplish whatever I have achieved in my life, I stood on my parents' shoulders, who stood on their parents' shoulders, and so on. In

2011, I was considered for one of the twenty most outstanding men of Springfield, Missouri. One of the questions that I was asked was, "If you could spend twenty-four hours as anyone—real or fictional, alive or dead—who would you choose and why?"

I did not have to think long before I knew my answer. I said, "I would spend twenty-four hours as myself and simply enjoy a day with my parents who passed away years ago. I would go back to a time when they were young and vibrant and express my appreciation and gratitude for all that they sacrificed for me and my brothers and sisters."

Their sacrifices made it possible for me to achieve the American dream. Thank you, Mom, Dad, and Papaw.

Let the wise listen and add to their learning, and let the discerning get guidance (Pr. 1:5).

Chapter 1

A Dream of a New Business

For whoever finds me finds life and receives favor from the Lord (Pr. 8:35).

As I was walking one evening and meditating on God's blessings on our business, I began to hear a voice that I recognized, speaking to me softly. He said, "Your goals are too small."

I said, "Okay, Lord, what is your goal for me?"

He replied, "Look up." I looked skyward to see a beautiful starry night in the Ozarks. He said, "Observe My creativity. Can you count the stars? That is how many units I want you to have. I want you to build a business that will impact your family for generations."

The dream of having a business began in the 1970s. Little did I know back then all that God had in store for our family. While in church listening to a guest speaker, Bob Buess, I became intrigued with this gifted man. Brother Buess exercised the gift of prophecy and would occasionally ask someone in the congregation to stand and receive a word of "personal prophecy." To my surprise, he chose me. I stood and listened as he said, "You are shooting your arrows too low. They are going into the ground. You must aim higher."

I did not know what this word of knowledge meant, but I intended to find out. Brother Buess went on and talked about the favor of the Lord and said that we should all seek God's favor.

He said that favor changes our insecurity into self-confidence and that God brings us into favor with Himself and man. He spoke of favor being the road to success and that it changes homes, husbands, wives, and children.

This kind of favor with God flows naturally to those who love Him with all of their hearts, minds, and souls. He said that if we seek the Lord with all of our hearts, we would surely find Him. He encouraged the congregation to confess favor with God and man and to reject the past as a rule for future living.

I knew that I needed favor in order to achieve my goals in life. Brother Buess encouraged each of us to confess favor every day of our lives. I decided to seek favor and believe that God would grant me this request.

> *Give, and it will be given to you. A good measure, pressed down, shaken together and running over, will be poured into your lap. For with the measure you use, it will be measured to you* (Lk. 6:38).

The Gift of Giving

This same minister also spoke on the so-called motivational gifts and mentioned the gift of giving (Romans 12:7). I remember thinking that I would like to have that gift and offered this thought as a prayer. Brother Buess then said, "Always coupled with the gift of giving is the gift of earning. In order to give it, you must first earn it."

My wife and I were college music teachers. I did not know how we would ever be able to earn a lot of money while remaining teachers. We were comfortable on our salaries, and we always gave as generously as we could, but somehow I sensed that this gift that I had just prayed for would only be fully realized when we were able to make more money.

I have hidden your word in my heart that I might not sin against you (Ps. 119:11).

I delight in your decrees; I will not neglect your word (Ps. 119:16).

Reading God's Word

Another speaker who had an influence on my development and growth was Phillip Green. This brother spoke on the importance of reading the Bible. He said that although *study* of scripture is important, the *reading* of God's Word is mentioned more times in the Bible. Brother Green read the entire Bible every two weeks. I began a program of reading through the Bible, and although there have been dry spells when I allowed the time pressures of life to crowd out my Bible reading, I have continued reading through it regularly.

I began by reading the Bible once a year. A few years ago, our pastor challenged us to read the Bible twice that year. I decided to stay with reading the Old Testament once a year, but I felt that I could read the New Testament twice in a year. At the half-year point, I had read the New Testament in six months. I thought, *That wasn't so hard. I want to read the Old Testament twice this year, as well as the New.* I finished the Old Testament in a month in order to catch up with the New. I proceeded to read the entire Bible once a month for the next year.

> *I delight in your decrees; I will not neglect your word. Do good to your servant, and I will live; I will obey your word* (Ps. 119:16–17).

> *Your word is a lamp to my feet and a light for my path* (Ps. 119:105).

I believe that this practice develops wisdom and enables one to have the answers to life's questions. Successful people in any business must be problem solvers. If you want to get a promotion at your job, become a problem solver. In order to become a problem solver in every area of life, read God's Word.

Another speaker who had a profound influence on my vision of a real estate business was David Coppel. Brother Coppel was the brother of our pastor, Gale Coppel, and came to our church to speak on the biblical principles of giving. As he shared his testimony of his success in buying twenty-seven duplexes in Sacramento, California, I was inspired. His sound scripture-based teaching gave me a firm base on which to found the dream of a real estate business.

For nothing is impossible with God (Lk. 1:37).

Influence of Writers

In 1980, my wife and I decided to leave our teaching positions and go into the music ministry. Although the money was no better, the concentration on the ministry gave me the opportunity to grow as a person. I began to read self-help books, such as *Possibility Thinking* by Robert Schuller. I had read Norman Vincent Peale's book, *The Power of Positive Thinking* years before, and the writings of Dr. Schuller were a perfect companion for this book.

I began to realize that if I wanted to achieve my goal of being an earner who could then exercise the gift of giving, I had to change the way I thought. I would have to learn how to "not conform to the pattern of this world, but be transformed by the renewing of [my] mind" (Romans 12:1-2). I had always been a "glass is half empty" thinker. I needed to become a new man with a transformed mind. I read as many of Dr. Schuller's writings as I could.

One book that was particularly important in my development was *The Peak to Peek Principle*. The idea is that, when one is growing in their ability to dream and develop, one must climb the peak in front of them in order to peek at the next mountain to climb. I was learning to think big and dream big. I was learning to seek God's vision and direction for my life. My paradigm was changing, and I was beginning to be able to see situations through God's eyes. It was a new and exciting way to view life!

Another important book in my development, *How to Win*

Friends and Influence People by Dale Carnegie, became my textbook for learning how to change the way one is perceived by other people. I discovered that small things, such as smiling more, using people's names, writing down one's goals, and having a positive mental attitude could help me change my paradigm.

A Humorous Look at Paradigm Shifts

Not long ago, our church, James River Assembly of God, invited a unique minister to our pulpit. Michael Junior uses humor to spread the good news of the gospel. He shared that his humor comes from his ability to see words from several different perspectives. As an example, he used an experience he had while he visited a comedy club in New York City. This club prided itself on its tradition of allowing young comics to come and show what they could do.

On one such occasion, Michael and a group of comedians that included Jay Leno of "The Tonight Show," discussed an item in the news concerning an NFL football player suing the league that could probably yield a good joke, but no one could quite come up with a winner.

When asked what he thought, Michael saw an opportunity to show what he could do. Years of preparation met a moment of opportunity. "Let me see if I've got this straight," he began. "A professional football player was hit in the eye with a penalty flag thrown by a referee, and he lost the sight in his left eye and is suing the league for three hundred million dollars. Did I get that right?"

"Yes," Mr. Leno responded. "That's exactly right."

Michael quipped, as quick as a flash, "Well, all I can say is that he won't see half of it."

The ability to come up with this joke so fast was a result of Michael's habit of looking at words from several different perspectives. The comedian Yakov Smirnoff possesses the same ability to see things differently than the rest of the world and mine humor from these different paradigms. He tells of going to the grocery and noticing the powdered milk with instructions to just add water. He then saw the powdered orange drink with the same instructions to add water. He then passed the baby powder and thought, "What a great country."

He had a similar thought when he noticed a baby changing table in the public restroom of a restaurant in Branson, Missouri, where his theater is located. "Imagine a country that has a place where, if you don't like your baby, you can change them. What a great country!" What a clever mind and ability to see the world from a different perspective and see the humor that is there.

Seed Faith Giving

Another book that had a profound influence on my life was Oral Roberts' *Seed Faith Giving*. Dr. Roberts described the biblical concept of sowing and reaping. The basic premise is that if one wanted to reap corn, one planted corn. Whatever a man sows, that is what he also reaps (2 Cor. 9:6). If one desires a return on an investment of money, one must sow money. God has put into effect the law of reciprocity. I discovered that if one wants to be a giver, he must first give out of what he already has.

We had always been givers to our church, but we began to seek opportunities to give above and beyond, in offerings to deserving ministries, such as "The 700 Club" and missions.

Dr. Roberts told of people who would attend his seminars on "Seed Faith Giving" and learn to look for ideas, insights, dreams, and visions. After one such event, a gentleman returned to his home and searched his attic for anything that might have value. He found an old violin and took it to an appraiser. What he had found was a very valuable Stradivarius! Another gentleman dug out plans for a special fuel injection system he had been working on and obtained a patent on it. The Jeep Motor Company purchased his invention, and he received royalties on his creation.

For the...world runs after all such things, and your Father knows that you need them. But seek his kingdom, and these things will be given to you as well (Lk. 12:30–31).

Location, Location, Location

I knew that we did not have a valuable violin or an invention dealing with fuel injection, but we did have ideas, insights, dreams, and visions. One dream was to own a McDonald's restaurant franchise. We even found a lot that we thought would be the perfect location for our endeavor. After attempting to reach the McDonald's headquarters in St. Louis several times, we learned that this franchise could only be bought by someone who already owned one.

A few years later, McDonald's did come to our city, and they built their restaurant on the exact lot that we had chosen. We realized that if we could instinctively locate the perfect place for a McDonald's, then we could be successful in business ventures of other types. I later learned that McDonald's spends hundreds of thousands of dollars researching their locations. We felt that we already knew what they found out because we trusted God to give us ideas, insights, dreams, and a vision. Although we did not get the franchise, we had chosen the right lot. This gave us confidence in our business instincts.

For whoever finds me finds life and receives favor from the Lord (Pr. 8:35).

Contacts: You Know Someone Who Knows Someone

One idea that had an impact on my future was that, although I might not have contacts, I knew some who did. I began to write letters to three people that I thought could help me with my career path, and each letter led to an important contact. Through one of them, we were called to a position to be Minister of Music at Living Faith Center in Santa Barbara, California.

This move would be pivotal in the building of our business. We were able to purchase a home and resell it when we moved to Springfield, Missouri, four years later. This profit became a large part of the nest egg for the building of our business.

> *And as if this were not enough in your sight, Sovereign Lord, you have also spoken about the future of the house of your servant* (2 Sam. 7:19).

FAQ: How Do I Get Started?

When people ask me what I do, I answer that I build and manage apartments. They usually respond in one of two ways:

First, they may relate how they tried that once and do not understand how anyone can manage rental units and deal with tenants. In most cases, those unhappy landlords either inherited a single-family house from their parents or other relative, or they bought a house at a great price and ultimately hated the experience.

When I inquire further, I discover that they made several key errors in their approach to management. They had failed to screen their prospective residents, failed to evict a delinquent resident, and/or failed to maintain the houses properly. These unhappy landlords would eventually sell the unit and vow never to own investment property again.

The second group responds by eagerly asking, "How did you get started?" I give a brief summary of my experience and encourage them to find a three-bedroom, two-bath, two-car garage house and get their real estate career started.

Sometime later, as I see these people in social situations and inquire about their real estate investments, some of them respond that they have thought about it a lot but are waiting for the right time. Unfortunately, the right time never seems to come for most of them.

You can come up with many creative reasons not to start your real estate investment career, but there is one big reason to begin—when you do, you are one step closer to your goal of financial independence. Perhaps, like Carol and myself, you are looking for something to augment your retirement income or you just want extra income for sending your child through college. Whatever your financial goals, you must get started.

It is said that Thomas Edison experimented with over 10,000 ways to create the incandescent light bulb. When asked if he was not discouraged after so many failures, he responded, "No, I am not discouraged in the least. I now know 10,000 ways in which it will not work." Dexter Yeager of Amway fame wrote a book entitled, *Don't Let Anyone Steal Your Dream*. The person most likely to steal your dream is yourself through procrastination.

There is a Chinese adage that a trip of 1,000 miles begins with a single step. Even in our fast-paced lives of travel by car, train, ship, or plane, that statement is still true. In business, one must begin with a single step. Many times that first step must be accomplished through a leap of faith.

Faith by itself, if it is not accompanied by action, is dead (Jas. 2:17).

Some years ago, I met a couple who lived at one of our apartment communities. They graciously invited me to breakfast to pick my brain regarding real estate investment. They shared that they had spent $10,000 on educational materials, seminars, and tapes in an attempt to learn how to invest in real estate.

Continuing education is a good thing, but if you want to start a real estate business, at some point you must buy a unit instead of investing in another "how-to" book or CD. The couple possessed as much knowledge as anyone I ever encountered, but they lacked the courage to step out and purchase a real estate unit.

I attended, via audio, a seminar conducted by Dr. Robert Schuller. He said that getting started was being half-finished and gave the following example:

Dr. Schuller was doing some yard work at his home in Garden Grove, California. He wanted to remove the dirt from the very front of his lawn and put in a nice ground cover. He loaded one wheelbarrow full of dirt and hauled it to his backyard. As he dumped the dirt into a pile he was starting, he began to realize how big this pile of dirt would become before he finished the job. He believed in "possibility thinking," and he prayed for help.

As he was loading his second wheelbarrow full of dirt, one of his parishioners drove by and asked what he was doing. He told him, and at that moment, a minor miracle began to unfold. The man was a contractor who needed a load or two of dirt just a couple blocks away from Dr. Schuller's home, and he told him he would take the dirt off his hands. The gentleman removed the dirt with his small bulldozer, put it in his dump truck, and hauled it away. This all happened within an hour or so.

A neighbor, who had seen him struggling to move the first wheelbarrow of dirt earlier, came home after running a few errands. Dr. Schuller was leisurely sweeping the dirt off of the sidewalk that the truck had left after it hauled away the load of dirt. The neighbor rolled down his window and asked, "How did you get that dirt moved so fast?"

Dr. Schuller responded, "I believe in possibility thinking!" This little miracle would not have happened if Dr. Schuller had not started. The apostle James said it best: Faith without action is dead.

FAQ: Am I Too Old to Start a Business?

In the same audio seminar mentioned above, Dr. Schuller told of a lady who had a desire to go back to school and get her education degree. She wanted to teach young people but was afraid that she was too old to begin the program. "It is a four-year program. I am 44 years old. Do you realize that I will be 48 in four years when I complete the degree?" she asked.

"How old will you be in four years if you do not go back to school and earn your degree?" Dr. Schuller replied.

Carol and I were 44 years old when we started TLC Properties. We are currently in our 25th year of business. If we had not started our business when we did, we would just be 25 years older now than when we began our company.

Harlan Sanders was 69 years old when he started Kentucky Fried Chicken. He was not a passive owner at that age. He would go to every new restaurant and personally train the staff on how to fry chicken his way. One is never too old to start a new business. Having a dream and a vision for a new business, with achievable goals and objectives, keeps one young.

FAQ: How Did You and Your Wife Go From Teaching Music to Multifamily Development?

We made the transition methodically and carefully over a period of years. We kept our college teaching jobs and music ministry positions for eight years after we started TLC Properties. We took no pay from TLC Properties during those eight years and put all of the earnings of the business back into the building of our real estate portfolio.

We also tried to use everything we had learned in our academics in the establishment of our business. We discovered a great deal of overlap between the world of music and the world of real estate.

I jokingly tell people who ask me how I purchased my first rental property that I had a chance to buy a nice house for a song, and because of my musical background, I had one. In truth, the first rental unit is almost always the most difficult. Taking that leap of faith and putting your money and reputation on the line can prove to be the hardest thing you have ever done. Remember that starting is being half-finished.

Unless the Lord builds the house, its builders labor in vain (Ps. 127:1).

Chapter 2

Getting Serious

I do not remember when we first became serious about the idea of owning a real estate business. I do remember reading several books on real estate investment in Santa Barbara, where we lived from 1982–86. I had also been inspired years before by David Coppel and the real estate investment business that he had developed in Sacramento, California.

When we first moved to Santa Barbara, we leased a home for a year. The rent was high for that time; I recall that it cost us $2,000 to get into this rental house. We had to pay first and last month's rent plus a security deposit. We had purchased our first home in Poplar Bluff for a down payment of $400, and that came from the four month's rent we had already paid since moving into the house.

When our lease came up for renewal, the landlord was going to raise the rent by $80 per month so we decided to buy a house if we could find one in our price range. We were fortunate to be able to buy a house in Goleta for $119,000 from a church member. Using our savings, we were able to get an FHA loan at a 10% interest rate. To get this lower rate (at that time), we did a fifteen-year amortization. The loan paid down faster, but this created a strain on our budget.

To help our financial situation, I requested that Carol be paid for her organ and piano playing at the church. I also took a position at Santa Barbara City College, conducting the Camerata Choir. This group sang oratorios such as "The German Requiem" by Brahms, "The Magnificat" by J.S. Bach, "Judas Maccabaeus" by Handel, and "The Messiah" by Handel.

Ask and it will be given to you; seek and you will find; knock and the door will be opened to you. For everyone who asks receives; he who seeks finds; and to him who knocks, the door will be opened (Mt. 7:7–8).

Our First Attempt

After successfully acquiring our home, Carol and I made an effort to buy an investment property. We found that everything was so expensive that it was impossible to make the income-to-debt ratio work so we could at least cover the mortgage and expenses. Shortly thereafter, however, a fortunate turn of events brought us to Springfield, Missouri, to be teachers at Evangel University.

This turn of events did not seem so fortunate at first. In November 1985, I was called into the pastor's office for a little chat. He informed me that my music program was dead and that if it did not get better fast, he would have to make a change. His tone was rather terse, and I felt as if I had just been fired. Strangely enough, he asked me not to tell my wife. I thought, *She may begin to wonder what's going on when I sell our house and move to another job.* I did inform Carol, and we both felt that we would be moving in the near future.

The church had a big 25th anniversary celebration coming in February 1986, and the pastor thought it would be awkward for him to be without a music director during these activities so I stayed on until the summer of 1986.

In March of that same year, we were offered positions at a new college being established in Tacoma, Washington, and so we proceeded accordingly. However, in May, I received a call from this college informing me that they were moving the school to Pleasanton, California, and would not open the campus for another year. I informed them that my position in Santa Barbara was gone and that I would have to look for another job.

> *I lift up my eyes to the hills—where does my help come from? My help comes from the Lord, the Maker of heaven and earth* (Ps. 121:1–2).

I Cry Out to God for Help

On the Monday after getting this news about the lack of a position, I had the day off and was walking on the beach, praying. Through tears, I cried out to God: "I need a job! I have a wife and three growing boys. Please, Lord! Help me!" Once again, the voice that I had heard before spoke to my heart and assured me that I would soon hear something that would give me hope.

We did not know what to do. Should we wait, or should we take action? Almost always, my instinct was to take action. "Do something; even if it is wrong," was my motto. I decided to call a contact. L.B. "Bud" Larsen was Director of the Music Department at the Assembly of God headquarters in Springfield, Missouri. I met him in 1979 at a music seminar in Springfield, and he had helped me get the jobs in Santa Barbara and Tacoma.

I explained to Brother Larsen what had happened, and he informed me that Evangel College was looking for a voice teacher. He told me to call Mr. John Shows, who was the chairman of the music department. I knew John Shows and immediately gave him a call. He told me that the position was still open, and he promised me that he would look at my credentials. He sounded interested, and Carol and I took heart from this conversation.

I sensed that the timing of this might well be the answer to my prayer on the beach just days earlier. I felt that God had heard my prayer, and my fervent cry for help had received an immediate response. I recalled the verse in Romans, which says that "suffering produces perseverance; perseverance, character; and character, hope" (Romans 5:3–4). I learned from my New Testament Literature professor, Dr. Wave Nunnally, that the Greek word for hope actually means "an absolute certainty."

This trial of getting fired had begun in November and lasted until May. We had lost one position due to a change in plans at the college, and we were ready for the hope (an absolute certainty) that Paul spoke of in Scripture.

Within days, Carol and I were in Springfield, interviewing for positions. We liked the situation, and they liked us. We got the jobs and began to plan our move to the Midwest. The idea of rearing our boys in the buckle of the Bible Belt especially appealed to us.

Whoever finds me finds life and receives favor from the Lord. But whoever fails to find me harms himself (Pr. 8:35–36a).

Go East, Young Man

We left Santa Barbara for Springfield in June. Traveling with three boys had never been easy, but we were prepared this time. Thanks to a friend of ours who worked at Santa Barbara Research, we were able to rig a video cassette player and a television so that the boys could watch movies in the back of our Toyota minivan.

This van, which looked somewhat like a pregnant roller skate, had a back seat that folded out to make a bed that was big enough for two boys. It had a captain's chair in the middle that swiveled and left enough space on the floor for fun and games. The Sylvester Stallone movie, *Rocky IV*, had become their favorite, and by the time we arrived in Springfield, I had the entire sound track of the movie memorized.

Everything was going well until we stopped for gas in Needles, California, and opened the side door of our van. Suddenly, a blast of hot air flooded into the back, and it felt as if we were standing in front of an oven with the door open. After all, we were in the middle of the Mojave Desert. Our son Daniel asked, "What's that?"

Carol explained that it was very hot here. "Then why are we leaving Santa Barbara?" he asked, rather disgusted.

While en route, we made a stop at the Grand Canyon. As we stood in awe of this wonder of the world, Daniel asked, "Is this all there is?" Later, he explained that he was expecting an amusement park, such as Six Flags or Disneyland or even Knott's Berry Farm. We could not fathom anyone being disappointed by the Grand Canyon. When we heard Daniel's explanation, we understood that it just was not what he had expected.

To you I will give the land of Canaan (1 Ch. 16:18a).

The Buckle of the Bible Belt

We finally arrived in Springfield and thanks to the investment in our home in California (the house in Goleta that we only pursued buying because our rent was about to go up $80 per month), we were able to purchase a dream home in a good neighborhood in the southeast part of town.

We refinanced the rental house we owned in Poplar Bluff, Missouri. This house had been our home, but in 1980 when we had moved from there, interest rates were at 17%, and since we could not sell the house, we had turned it into a rental. This refinance yielded $30,000 in equity.

I began to see if I owned ten houses that could be refinanced, I could pull $300,000 in equity out of these units. I also saw that investment in real estate was clearly a numbers business. The more units one owned, the more money one could make when they sold or refinanced the properties. I began to get excited about building a real estate business in Springfield.

The boys had given up the Pacific Ocean and Goleta Beach, which were only minutes from our home in Goleta. They insisted that, at the very least, we have a home with a pool. We settled on a neighborhood pool, and they were happy.

Listen to my instruction and be wise; do not ignore it. Blessed is the man who listens to me, watching daily at my doors, waiting at my doorway. For whoever finds me finds life and receives favor from the Lord (Pr. 8:33–35).

Start Small and Grow

After getting settled into our new home, I began to look for houses that I thought would work as investments. To my surprise, good opportunities were everywhere. I found that one could buy a nice three bedroom house in a good neighborhood for under $50,000. In Santa Barbara, this same house would have cost $150,000 or more.

It was not long until I had my real estate license and was making an offer on a nice three bedroom home not far from our residence. This house was a "For Sale by Owner" or FSBO. The couple selling the house had an FHA loan that was only assumable by a first-time homebuyer. Since we did not qualify for this program, we would need to find another way to buy it.

Carol loved this house, which backed onto a city-maintained park, had three bedrooms, one bath, and a one-car garage. It was in a nice neighborhood and just minutes from our home.

The sellers agreed to allow me to list the house. I then purchased the house through my own listing. We were able to use the 6% commission on the sale as part of our cash down-payment on the purchase. We had now bought our first house, which was specifically for investment purposes, but we still owned our former home in Poplar Bluff and kept it rented.

We put about $2,000 of our own money into this deal, but I received about $2,400 in commissions for both listing and selling the house. The exciting aspect of this deal was that about five years later, we were able to trade our equity in this unit ($15,000) for a twelve-unit apartment building located on East Cherry Street.

So in everything, do to others what you would have them do to you, for this sums up the Law and the Prophets (Mt. 7:12).

FAQ: Should I Invest in Single-Family Homes or Multifamily Apartments?

In the beginning of your real estate investment career, buying single-family homes makes sense. Everyone lives in homes at some point in their life. They have a familiarity with single-family homes, and there is a comfort level that may not exist with multifamily units. Therefore, we recommend that you begin with a nice house in a good area, rent it to a qualified tenant, and see how you like the experience.

Some people do not enjoy dealing with rentals, and if this is the case, you will want to discover this truth sooner, rather than later. You do not want to purchase an expensive apartment building only to find out that you hate the real estate investment business.

If the first experience works well, repeat the process in another neighborhood that is not far away. We are all busy, and the close proximity of rental houses will save time. If this second purchase seems to work well for you, seek out and buy a third rental and see how that feels.

If, after the purchase of three rental units, you are still hungry for more, it may be time to take a look at multifamily developments. I would recommend that you start small and grow. Begin with a duplex or a four-unit building that is in a good area of town.

The location criteria for your multifamily portfolio will be different than your single-family rentals. You want apartments that are near major arterial streets but not on them. You want them to be located near a large supermarket and a bus stop. Close proximity to shopping and restaurants is a nice bonus.

You will find that the single-family rentals are easier to

buy, but there is less positive cash flow in the transaction. Multifamily units are more difficult to purchase, due to the cost, but there is more cash flow available when you have several units under one roof. Perhaps a balance between the two is a good goal in the beginning years of your business. Buying multifamily units, however, will propel your business to greater earnings than single-family homes, and apartments are easier to maintain. Whatever direction you decide to go, you will be successful if you do your due diligence each step of the way.

FAQ: How Do I Find Good Rental Investments?

When we were looking for our first rental unit in Springfield, we began by looking in areas that we liked and that were close to our home in the southeast part of town. We read the newspaper's classified ads, drove around the area, and toured all open houses that we could before we bought. If we had not taken that step, we would still be in the same position that we were, only we would be 25 years older.

We were primarily interested in three-bedroom houses with two baths in good neighborhoods. Remember that the three most important things in real estate are: location, location, and location. When we found good rentals that met all or most of our criteria, we acted. The apostle Peter had to first get out of the boat before the miracle of walking on water could occur.

FAQ: Why Is Location So Important in Real Estate Investment?

There are many reasons why location is so important in real estate, but the best one is that location is the only aspect of real estate that cannot be changed. There are some other reasons for carefully selecting your locations.

The best place to find good rental houses is in an area of owner-occupied homes. You want to own the only rental house in the neighborhood. Owner-occupied homes are better maintained than rental houses. You also want to own the least expensive house in the area that blends in with the more expensive homes around it. You want to be in an area where the value of the neighborhood homes raises the value of your home, not vice versa.

Another important consideration is the schools in the area of your rental. Tenants who are looking for a nice rental and have school-aged children will ask about the neighborhood schools. Know the schools and their reputations before you purchase a rental house in that area.

Remember my rule of thumb regarding location. If I cannot walk down the street at night with my wife and family and feel safe, I do not purchase in that area. As you look at neighborhoods, walk several blocks around the house you are considering, and do the same test. There are communities where urban blight is encroaching on a neighborhood but has not reached the area of the particular house. You must think ahead and ascertain what that neighborhood will look like in five or ten years. This is particularly important if you are going to hold your units for several years rather than resell quickly.

Chapter 3

TLC Properties Is Born

We had now officially started our real estate investment business. Carol liked the name, TLC Properties, for our business. We decided to endeavor to exhibit the traits of tender love and care to our residents.

We desired to treat everyone that we met in our business—regardless of the relationship—like we would want to be treated if the situations were reversed. This remains a mainstay of our business philosophy. The "Golden Rule" is our company's slogan.

Not long after we bought this rental house, the furnace broke down. The house had a window air conditioning unit, which we did not like so we decided to replace the furnace and put a central air conditioning unit in at the same time. This cost money, and we would not have spent it if it were not necessary.

This upgrade of the heating and cooling system proved to be a valuable asset for the house. It was easy to rent with this new heating and cooling system, and its value increased when we traded it a few years later.

We then purchased another three-bedroom house from a faculty colleague, who was moving to another job. I looked at it, and although it had only a one-car garage and only one and a half baths, I decided to buy it because the terms were so good. Our faculty friend had an FHA loan, which was fully assumable for a modest fee. After all closing costs and the down payment, we were able to purchase that three-bedroom home for $1,500 in out-of-pocket expenses.

We immediately leased this house by placing a sign in the yard. One of the tenants, who had handyman skills, constructed a metal outbuilding in the backyard. When his family moved out after four years, we found that he had allowed his dog to have free run of the house. We had to change the carpet, which was expensive, but the upgrade proved to be a boon. We were able to keep the house fully leased during the five years we owned it. One young couple, who looked at the house, really wanted to buy it, and we sold it to them for several thousand dollars more than we paid for it by carrying a second deed of trust. The young couple paid off that second within a year. The biggest factor in their wanting to buy the house was that they loved the new carpet. We were able to pocket about $5,000 for the time and energy that we had expended during our five years of ownership.

Choose my instruction instead of silver, knowledge rather than choice gold, for wisdom is more precious than rubies, and nothing you desire can compare with her (Pr. 8:10–11).

Our Third House: The Sweet Spot

I had read in several books on real estate investments that the ideal rental was a three bedroom, two bath house with a two car garage. We bought a new house in southwest Springfield and leased it to a minister associate of Carol's.

This unit met every criterion that we had desired. It had three bedrooms, two complete baths, a two-car garage, and was in a good neighborhood, which had excellent public schools. The price was $56,900 and the seller agreed to carry a 10% second and pay all closing costs up to $2,000.

The bank agreed to loan us 80% of the price ($45,520), and I was able to use my 3% commission as the selling agent to reduce the down payment by another $1,700. Our out-of-pocket expenses on this house were about $4,000.

At closing, the seller offered to pay us $300 in unused closing monies, but we decided to apply the money to the principle on the second deed of trust. We sold this house eight years later for $70,000 and made a profit of about $25,000. The house stayed leased the entire term of our ownership.

These three buys came in rapid succession and were all leased almost as soon as we bought them. We simply had some professionally painted signs made with our phone number on them and placed them in the front yard.

We now owned four rental houses, including the house we still owned in Poplar Bluff and had kept as a rental since we left in 1980. Owning rental property from a distance challenged us, especially when we lived in California. However, we managed in part thanks to our attorney back in southeast

Missouri, Mr. Norman Chadwick, who had also been our neighbor when we lived there.

> *Blessed is the man who finds wisdom, the man who gains understanding, for she is more profitable than silver and yields better returns than gold* (Pr. 3:13–14).

Cash Flow: Positive and Negative

Our new business was off to a solid start. Our positive cash flow on these three rental houses was $195 per month. Remember the adage: "Despise not small beginnings." We felt that we had just begun and that the cash flow would come. We still had our day jobs, so cash flow was not our most important goal. We intended to build a business over the long run and wanted to add to our portfolio without much concern for cash flow.

One rule we did adhere to was to pass on any property that caused a negative cash flow. We did not have the capital necessary to offset any large negative cash flows. As long as the rental unit made money, we felt good about it, even if the amount was only ten dollars per month.

I had read that even if one's negative cash flow was $50 per month, one would reach a limit on how many of these situations that could be handled. On the other hand, if each unit produced a positive cash flow of $50, one's ability to handle this situation would be infinite if the sole consideration was cash flow.

> *The path of the righteous is like the first gleam of dawn, shining ever brighter till the full light of day* (Pr. 4:18).

We Find Our Niche

As I scoured the classified ads for houses, I could not avoid seeing the ads for multifamily housing for sale. I was fascinated by the possibility of adding several units to our portfolio at one time, in one transaction, and all on the same site. I began to call the realtors and inquire about the various offerings.

One realtor showed us three nice properties: a sixteen-unit building, an eleven-unit building, and a twelve-unit building. I wanted to buy them all, but the wise realtor asked, "Do you think you could borrow the money for all three?" That thought had never entered my mind. We were teachers with a rock solid credit rating. I believed, erroneously, that banks would line up to loan us money. We had a lot to learn about borrowing money from banks.

I learned that the going rate for good locations and well-maintained apartments was around $25,000 per unit. The agent who had shown me the first three apartment communities called me one day and told me about a ten-unit building he had just listed, which was located not far from our home.

Make level paths for your feet and take only ways that are firm. Do not swerve to the right or the left; keep your foot from evil (Pr. 4:26–27).

We Take the Plunge Into Multifamily

I liked the idea of owning rental units close to where we lived. Since we were managing them ourselves, having every unit within easy driving distance was a time-saving asset. The owner of these apartments had built them himself and wanted to build more units on the north side of Springfield. He had put a lot of sweat equity into these apartments and was ready to move on and do the same thing on land he had recently purchased.

We bought Southern Hills Apartments, as we named the ten units, for $227,000. We asked the seller to carry a $27,500 second deed of trust with a seven-year balloon payment. The interest rate on the second was a reasonable 8%. We split the 6% brokerage fee with the listing agent for selling the property to us and received an 80% loan from the bank.

The first bank we approached for the opportunity to loan us the money on this project turned us down. We then went to the bank that had financed the project for the seller, and they agreed to the loan. I learned not to give up when one bank turned me down. The persistence paid off with an approved loan from the second bank.

We had our first multifamily community and put only $9,200 of our capital reserves into the transaction. That was a cost of $920 per unit. We were able to make $500 per month positive cash flow and get our original investment back in eighteen months.

I did not know it, but a wonderful sequence of events had been put into motion. The positive and profitable results that would ensue from this one purchase proved to be unbelievable. God's ways are truly amazing.

"For I know the plans I have for you," declares the Lord, "plans to prosper you and not to harm you, plans to give you hope and a future" (Jer. 29:11).

A Family Business Develops

It did not take long to realize that this was our niche. We loved our nine one-bedroom and one three-bedroom apartment community. In the beginning, we did everything ourselves to save money. My sons helped, and although they say that they were slave labor, I paid them for their help. We mowed the yard, cleaned the carpets, scrubbed the bathrooms, made repairs, and everything else involved in managing the units. If we had a repair that we could not handle, we called the appropriate professional and used them as subcontractors.

When we had a vacancy, we placed a professionally painted "For Rent" sign in the front yard. When we received a call, one of us drove the short distance to the property and met the prospect.

At first, we did much of our screening by instinct. We were fortunate to have had only a few bad tenants. We learned later to do credit checks and get references. By this time, TLC Properties was only three months old, and we already had three houses and a ten-unit apartment community. We were off to a solid beginning.

To the faithful you show yourself faithful, to the blameless you show yourself blameless, to the pure you show yourself pure, but to the crooked you show yourself shrewd (2 Sa. 22:26–27).

We Prove Ourselves

Mr. Howard Williams, who owned the property across the street from our ten units, contacted me one day in the fall of 1991 and asked if we would like to buy his eight two-bedroom units. It had taken us three years to show this gentleman that we knew what we were doing. I looked at them and said that we were interested. He was adamant on his price ($220,000), but we wanted to protect our investment capital.

After going back and forth for about a year, we were able to buy the property for a price of $212,500 and only had to put $12,500 down. Even better, the seller agreed to carry the $200,000 mortgage at 9% interest—a reasonable rate at the time (1992). Our cash into this transaction was $12,500 or $1,562 per unit. Because this seller was carrying the mortgage, he had to be sure that we would succeed. He did not want to take the property back.

When we did finally settle on the deal, we had eight two bedrooms, which proved to be the perfect complement for our one-bedrooms just across the street. The maintenance was easier due to the close proximity of the two communities.

Dishonest money dwindles away, but he who gathers money little by little makes it grow (Pr. 13:11).

A Twelve-Unit Community

About a year later, Mr. Williams called to see if we would be interested in buying a twelve-unit building just minutes from the location of our existing units. I looked at these one-bedroom units and liked them. The best part of this deal was, once again, the terms.

We were able to trade the equity in one of our rental houses (the first one we had bought, which backed up to a city park) for a big part of the down payment. Even more important was the seller's willingness to carry the entire mortgage at 8% interest. Because he had seen our success over the past five years, he was willing to carry almost half a million dollars in mortgages on the two properties.

I recently talked with Mr. Williams and his wife on the telephone about a political meeting we were having at our house. I found out that he was living in Scottsdale, Arizona, because of all the notes he carried when he sold his apartment buildings. He proved that there are many ways to make money in real estate. Howard Williams and his wife make money through real estate that they sold years ago. They earn this money while living the good life in Arizona.

The sale price on this apartment community was $300,000. The loan was $265,000. The equity in our rental house that we traded was $15,000 (the first one we bought). Our cash into this project was about $20,000 or about $1,667 per unit. After owning this property for four years, we were able to sell it for $31,000 more than we paid for it and use that money to purchase land for a new apartment development on the west side of town.

You will be made rich in every way so that you can be generous on every occasion, and through us your generosity will result in thanksgiving to God (2 Co. 9:11).

Our Goal: How About $1,000,000 in Debt?

Our goals were to own one hundred units and to be $1,000,000 in debt. My theory was that when we paid off the debt, we would be millionaires. When I shared this idea with a good friend, Jim Brown, he thought I was crazy. The idea of a business strategy based on being $1,000,000 in debt was foreign to him.

We had now acquired thirty-six units. We didn't know it, but a fortunate chain of events was about to propel our five-year-old business into rapid growth.

As my family and I were mowing the yard at the ten-unit community we had purchased in July 1988, I began to wonder if the city would allow us to build a four-unit building on the west side of the lot. I quickly got our survey out of storage and went down to the City Planning Department and asked if this was possible.

The City Planning director informed me that there was an old pipeline buried under the west corner of the lot, and there was an easement that would not allow a building to be erected on that part of the lot. This easement, however, would allow a parking lot.

Carol wondered if we could build on another part of the lot that was a parking lot and had no easement. The plan would be to expand the parking over the easement and put a four-unit building on part of the parking lot on the east side of the property. We would then expand the parking on the west side over the easement to make up for the lost parking and give us enough parking for the four new units.

Once again, I took the survey to the city planner, and

after some careful thought, he agreed. We had the green light to build. Our first task would be hiring a builder. We knew who to turn to for help.

Unless the Lord builds the house, its builders labor in vain (Ps. 127:1).

We Hire a Builder

We hired a builder, our acquaintance Don Chadwick, who had built and sold us the ten-unit community. He was perfect for the job since he knew this lot well. He was an excellent builder and had been the general contractor on several apartment buildings in Springfield.

Hiring Don as our general contractor ensured us that banks would not hold our inexperience against us. Don had plenty of experience and all of the banks knew and respected him.

Don agreed to do the project for a modest 5% fee based on the overall value of the building. We learned later that the standard rate for a general contractor was 10%.

Not only was Don constructing our building, but he was also training me to do the same in the future. He proved invaluable in the entire experience. He assisted in the hiring of the architect, getting the plans approved by the city, and eventually getting a permit.

We began construction in November 1993 and finished the project in February 1994. If there is a worse time to try and rent units in Springfield, Missouri, than the middle of winter, I have not yet found it. Carol and I worked hard on this building. We did most of the cleaning ourselves, including the final clean. We were so proud of this project. It had become our "baby."

Commit to the Lord whatever you do, and your plans will succeed (Pr. 16:3).

Our "Baby," The Barn

Our "baby" looked like a barn, but to us, it was the prettiest four-unit building we had ever seen. By opening day, the building was filled, and the rents were higher than the existing units. We learned quickly that *new* was the way to go. This principle proved hard for us to learn, but some wise bankers helped us see this principle clearly.

The barn had cost $93,000 to complete. The bank had loaned us $78,000, and we had put about $15,000 of our own money into the project. The $3,750 per unit of out-of-pocket money may seem high, but these units were new and demanded higher rents than the existing units. We also received $2,000 in rents and deposits before we opened. These units were much less expensive to maintain because they were new.

We had taken a big step of faith, and God was faithful to help us. God's servant, Don Chadwick, became our mentor and friend during this construction. He had come along beside us and helped us achieve our dream. Don enjoyed the building process (the smell of sawdust, the sound of the saws and hammers), but he was also an excellent teacher.

Don was as eager to share his knowledge with me as I was to learn. I tried to soak up every bit of knowledge that I could. I knew that I would soon be building on my own. I needed the knowledge that Don possessed in order to continue our dream of building our real estate investment company. We almost got sidetracked with a tempting project near our other properties. It had 144 units, and although we only had forty units at the time, we bravely rushed in where angels would surely fear to tread. Fortunately, circumstances kept us from making a big mistake.

Teach me your way, O Lord; lead me in a straight path (Ps. 27:11a).

The California Club Apartments

We had purchased thirty-six units and built four units. We didn't know it, but we had only just begun; the best was yet to come. We began to expand our vision and looked for larger apartment communities to purchase.

One such development, The California Club, was advertised in the classified section. I drove by and looked at it; and although it was older, it was in a great location and had nice amenities. This community was an even mix of one- and two-bedroom units. They were asking $2,900,000 ($20,139 per unit) and stated in the ad that it was a "steal." I thought it was priced to sell, based on my belief that units in Springfield—in good locations and well maintained—usually sold for about $25,000 a unit.

Get wisdom, get understanding; do not forget my words or swerve from them (Pr. 4:5–6).

Our Proposal

We used all of Carol's skill in writing our proposal (she was going to the University of Arkansas in pursuit of her doctorate) and submitted it to several local banks. They all politely said no. Again, they were concerned about our capital reserves. One of the bankers, David Thayer, gave us the bad news with regrets. He then said something profound.

"Sometimes 'no' is a good answer," he said. When I asked him to explain, he said, "Maybe the money you would have spent on this project will be available for a better opportunity that is just around the corner."

As we look back on this, we realize that God had a better idea. These apartments were old and needed some updating. God had another plan and one that was far better. He seemed to keep reminding us of what He taught us with the four-unit building. New is almost always better in multi-family development.

> *And afterward, I will pour out my Spirit on all people. Your sons and daughters will prophesy, your old men will dream dreams, your young men will see visions* (Joel 2:28).

The failure to acquire The California Club apartments—at first a big disappointment—became a blessing in disguise. Using the funds that we would have used on these units, we purchased land for a large development that would take our business to a new level. This development would push our total number of units beyond the 100 that had been our goal and set us on a course of growth that we could not have anticipated.

Praise God from whom all blessings flow,
Praise Him all creatures here below,
Praise Him above the heavenly hosts,
Praise Father, Son, and Holy Ghost. (Doxology).

FAQ: To Borrow or Not To Borrow?

A tenant in our office building, Bradford Place, asked to speak to me about investing in real estate. This gentleman, successful in his chosen field, wanted to build a business that would allow him to generate cash flow that was primarily self-sustained. He informed me that he had $200,000 to invest, and his real estate agent had located two nice homes that interested him. He intended to pay cash for these houses.

The first house was near a local college, and the list price was $47,000. The second house, located in southwest Springfield, was listed for $49,000. Both of these houses contained two bedrooms and one bath. The locations were good, and the prices seemed fair for the market.

I asked him if he had considered borrowing the money for these investments.

He answered, "No. I wanted to pay cash because I thought that would simplify the process."

I encouraged him to consider borrowing the money and proceeded to use the following example:

An investor in California had $100,000 to invest. Should he buy one house for the entire amount or ten houses by using leverage (borrowed money)? If he decides to buy one house, his equity position in five years, with a modest inflation rate of 2% annually, would be just over 10%, or a little over $10,000. Or should he buy ten houses by paying 10% down, asking the seller to carry a 10% second, and acquiring an 80% mortgage from the bank?

In both scenarios, the buyer invests $100,000. In the second example, however, his equity position is increased by a multiplication factor of ten. The investor's entire original nest egg is recaptured in five years. There are also tax incentives to take advantage of in the second case, namely the interest deductions on the mortgage payments. Leverage can become your best friend in real estate investing when you are prudent and use good, sound judgment.

Many people, whose parents or grandparents went through the great depression, believe that all debt is bad. The tenants, however, are repaying real estate investment mortgages. This is described as "good debt" in the real estate business.

Robert Schuller told the story in one of his seminars of attempting to borrow money for coal to heat his home. His banker explained to him that one cannot borrow money for coal because coal is a consumable commodity. If one defaults on the loan, there is nothing to repossess. Using borrowed money to buy coal is a bad debt, but accumulating debt to build a real estate business is a good debt. Banks gladly loan money for these types of endeavors to qualified borrowers.

FAQ: How Do I Borrow From Banks?

The most important thing to remember about borrowing money from banks is that they want to make good, sound loans. Your job is to convince them that you are a good risk. They must be absolutely convinced that you have the ability to repay the loan on time.

The first bank to go to when you need money to purchase a rental property is the one where you currently bank. Meet with one of their loan officers and explain what you want to accomplish with your investments. The loan officer will ask you to fill out a personal financial statement, which will show the bank your net worth (total assets minus all debts on those assets).

The bank will run a credit check to ascertain your credit worthiness. It is sometimes good to run your own credit report to see where you are. If your credit score is high (in the mid to high 700s) and your net worth is good, you have your foot in the door.

FAQ: How Do I Establish My Company With a Bank?

When we first started, our net worth was low, but our credit rating was high. Our capital reserves were also low, but we did not use the income from our rentals to live on; we kept our day jobs. The banks liked the fact that we were active in our church and in the community. These are what I call "intangible factors" that need to be high if you want to get the loan you are seeking.

What we lacked in financial strength, we tried to make up for in other areas. We produced the best proposals most bankers had ever seen. In other words, we tried to accentuate our positives while acknowledging our weaknesses. Remember, banks are in business to make loans. If the first one you try turns you down, go to another. When you finally find the bank that will loan you the money for your dream of a real estate investment business, move all of your banking business to that bank.

Establish a relationship with your banker that will last a

lifetime. Almost no one can build a real estate business without the help of a friendly banker.

Chapter 4

A Dream Begins To Be Realized

Upon completion of our first building project, I thought, *That wasn't so bad. I believe we can do that again!* After The California Club disappointment, I began looking for land that could be zoned for multifamily units. The plan was to build more four-unit buildings because that is what we had just built, and we felt comfortable with a project of this size.

I called a realtor who had a lot for sale near our twelve-unit building on East Cherry Street. Again, I valued the close proximity to our existing units. The agent informed me that the price of the parcel was $200,000 and that it contained four acres.

He proceeded to tell me of another parcel he had, which was perfect for what I wanted to build. "Everything is in," he said. "The detention, sewer, water, and electric are all there. There are eight lots and they are listed for $1.25 per foot. They are located in southwest Springfield near Kansas Expressway and Battlefield Road. They won't last long. This is a terrific location."

The Lord will keep you from all harm—he will watch over your life; the Lord will watch over your coming and going both now and forevermore (Ps. 121:7–8).

Listening to the Inner Voice

He might as well have said that they were located in Kansas. I was forming the words to tell him that I did not want to build units in southwest Springfield when something critical happened. A voice in my mind interrupted my train of thought and said, "Don't say no without looking." I stopped the words that I had almost said and instead responded, "I will go by and take a look at them."

I had heard this voice before at critical times in my life and recognized the prompting of the Holy Spirit of God. One of the first times I had felt the prompting of the Holy Spirit was in August 1971. We were returning home after four weeks of study in Amherst, Massachusetts. Carol, her brother, sister, her sister's friend, and I were on the New York freeway when we encountered an old truck going very slow in the left lane. I was reluctant to pass it, however, because signs all along the highway said, "Don't Pass on the Right."

I thought that the driver of the antique truck would eventually see us and move to the right. After what seemed like a long time, I decided to move to the right. I told my hands and arms to perform the act, but for some unknown reason, the steering wheel did not turn. It was as if the signal from my brain did not get sent, even though I wanted it to be sent.

As I thought about why my limbs would not obey, a car going well in excess of 100 miles per hour zoomed past our car on the right. If I had pulled into the right lane, we and the people in the speeding car would have been killed. Even the older people in the old truck would have been in jeopardy. I knew that the Holy Spirit, or one of His ministering angels, had kept my hands from turning that wheel.

Carol had developed a habit of praying for our safety every time we got in the car. "I plead the blood of Jesus over this car—bumper to bumper, side to side, top to bottom, and every working part," she always prayed. She later added the passengers in her safety prayer. I believe that on that day on a New York State freeway, her prayer of safety was in full operation.

God had mercifully spared our lives and the lives of all the offspring we would have who were riding with us. I calculated that there were over twenty-five people, theoretically, in our car when the offspring were counted.

For he will command his angels concerning you to guard you in all your ways (Ps. 91:11).

East Side, West Side, and all Around the Town

Everything we owned, except the one house we had bought for the pastor, was on the southeast side of town. We lived in that area, and everything was close. But God had a far, far better plan.

It was several days later before I drove to the southwest side of town. When I passed by these lots, there was only one thought in my mind, *A one-eyed monkey could make this work.* The realtor had not overstated the features of the property.

The location was perfect—close to major streets but not on them. The tract of land was one block away from a major north-south artery and a block and a half north of a major east-west artery.

The eight lots were about 30,000 square feet each, and the seller was asking $1.25 per foot. With the advice and counsel of my friend, Don Chadwick, I made a low offer ($.90 per foot), and to my surprise and delight, they accepted.

I was elated but decided that before I purchased the land, I should see if I could find a friendly banker who would loan me the money to build these units. After six banks rejected our proposal, we found one that agreed to finance the project. We were elated and eager to get started on our newest project. By the time I wrote my contract, one of the corner lots had already been sold to someone else. We would have to make it work with seven lots.

Delight yourself in the Lord and he will give you the desires of your heart (Ps. 37:4).

Capital Reserves

One of the banks that had turned us down said that our proposal was one of the finest they had ever received, but they were not going to make us the loan due to their concern about our capital reserves.

I could not disagree with the bank's assessment. We had started our new business with a nest egg of $62,000 (acquired from the sale of our Santa Barbara house and the refinance of our Poplar Bluff house), and although we had used about half of the money in our investments to date, we had enough money to buy two lots and finance the remainder.

We took most of our savings and paid $54,000 for the two lots. We had our savings in a mutual fund, and to our surprise, we were unable to get the money in time for the closing. We decided to use several credit cards to get the cash necessary to buy the acreage. When we told the realtor how we were going to purchase the lots, he looked at us like we were crazy.

The seller carried the mortgage on the remaining five lots at 7% interest paid quarterly, with the entire amount due in two years. The plan was to pay for the five remaining lots, one at a time, as we borrowed the money for each of the five remaining buildings to be built.

Lazy hands make a man poor, but diligent hands bring wealth (Pr. 10:4).

Is It a Hobby or a Business?

As Carol and I talked about the future of our business, we wondered what would happen to our real estate investment company and our management company if we were to treat these like business endeavors instead of hobbies.

We had both studied privately for years, gone to school and acquired three degrees from three universities, and dedicated ourselves to our educational goals, both as students and later as teachers. We made a decision that we would devote the same energy, thought, and dedication to this endeavor as we had to our academic pursuits. This decision would be the kick-start that the business needed to take it to the next level.

This is the day the Lord has made; let us rejoice and be glad in it (Ps. 118:24).

The Dream and the Academics Merge

We always felt that the thirty years we spent in teaching and church work were vital to our development as business people and developers. This belief would only be underscored as we moved forward in our business career.

Two years before we began to build, Carol decided to go back to school and complete her doctorate in college teaching. The knowledge and training that she received during this time proved to be most helpful in growing the business. We used her knowledge to write our proposal to the banks for a loan for our new apartment community.

When the proposal was finished, it was a thing of beauty. We had included a cover page, index, history of the business, personal resumes, and all of the projections of costs and rental income.

Again, we went to six banks, and all said a polite no.

One gentleman said, "Your proposal is one of the best I have ever seen, but we cannot finance the project."

I knew that we only needed one bank to say yes.

On our seventh attempt, we got the answer that we needed. The bank agreed to loan us 75% of the appraised value. We were serving as our own general contractor and using Don Chadwick as the builder. I had the green light and could hardly wait to get started on the construction.

Praise the Lord. Blessed is the man who fears the Lord, who finds great delight in his commands (Ps. 112:1).

Sunset Place Apartments Becomes a Reality

Using the capital we had from the sale of our home in Santa Barbara along with money we had saved, we bought the seven lots. For the first eight years of our new business, we took no pay for ourselves. We lived on our day jobs. We put everything that we could into expanding our business. We boldly asked the sellers to finance five of the lots and paid cash for two lots. The bank required that we construct one building at a time. When we had each building stabilized, they would finance another. We decided to scrub the idea of constructing four-unit apartment buildings and opted for sixteen-unit buildings in order to maximize the land.

The process of obtaining a permit took longer than I expected, but we broke ground in May 1994. Don Chadwick once again coached me, and I paid him 5% as before. When we began Sunset Place, Carol and I were still teaching and needed Don to oversee the job site. On weekends, we cleaned the site. I discovered that subcontractors are the sloppiest people in the world. I had never seen so much trash. It was a big job just to keep the units swept, but we made it a family project. The boys pitched in and helped, and I paid them a little for their labor.

In order to save some construction time, I found a second bank that agreed to finance the second building, and I was able to overlap construction. The first sixteen-unit building opened on a cold and breezy day in November of that same year. All but two of the sixteen units were leased. Evidently we had built apartments that people seemed to like.

The second building, along with an office and a pool and laundry facility, was completed in April 1995, and was fully leased right away. As we were completing the second building, I informed Don that I did not believe I needed him anymore. He jokingly accused me of firing him. I explained that his valuable teaching had prepared me to carry on by myself. He had worked himself out of a job. I thanked him for his help. On more than one occasion, I have told Don that we could not have built our company without him. We still keep in touch, and Don invariably enjoys talking shop. He loves the construction business and imparted that love and passion on to me.

Our Distinctive Emerges

We had hired a decorator to help us with our color selections, both inside and out, and she did a great job of selecting decors that people liked. We put in all the kitchen appliances (refrigerators with ice makers, electric ranges, microwave ovens, and dishwashers), and our two-bedroom units had two full baths. We also put washer-drier hookups in each unit. We emphasized storage space and built large closets. We tried to build with the woman's needs in mind and, therefore, built nice kitchens and large baths. These traits became our distinctive edge.

The third building opened in June 1995, and like the second one, was full. Building Four (a twelve-unit) opened in October 1995. We finished the community with openings in

May, July, and September of 1996. Each building was completely leased when it opened. When we finished the clubhouse in August 1996, we had 108 units (sixty one-bedroom units and forty-eight two-bedroom units) at what we named Sunset Place Apartments.

To our surprise and delight, the units were almost completely filled before we even opened them. Carol creatively used credit cards to borrow money to pay off subcontractors for the last buildings. She knew that we would be able to pay them off in six months.

We knew that we had made the right decision to build. The response to these new units was more than we could have hoped for. With Don Chadwick acting as our builder and advisor, we had constructed forty-eight units in one year. The remaining sixty units would follow during the next year. Sam Jr. became the first employee of TLC Properties in January 1996 and was the construction manager for the second phase, while acting as manager for the existing units.

A good man leaves an inheritance for his children's children (Pr. 13:22).

My Abraham Moment

Our goals had always been modest. We wanted to supplement our retirement income from the income of 100 units. We now had a total of 140 units. I had already overshot my goal.

As I mentioned in the beginning of this book, I was walking one evening in August 1996 and meditating on

God's blessings on our business when I began to hear a voice that I recognized, speaking to me softly. He said, "Your goals are too small."

I answered, "Okay, Lord, what is your goal for me?"

He replied, "Look up." I looked skyward to see a beautiful starry night in the Ozarks. He said, "Observe My creativity. Can you count the stars? That is how many units I want you to have. I want you to build a business that will impact your family for generations."

I had read once that one can count about six thousand stars on a clear night. I knew that this would take me the rest of my life to accomplish, but I accepted the challenge. Once again, the Holy Spirit was guiding me. From the beginning, we had prayed about this business. Before we bought our first apartment community, Carol and I prayed, and God spoke to us with encouraging—if not cautious—words. He said, "Go ahead, but be careful. There are sharks in the water." God was leading, and we were following. We were continuing to learn how to dream big.

FAQ: Should I Self-Manage or Hire a Management Company?

After Thomas Edison invented the light bulb, he knew that without a power plant to produce the electricity to operate the light, his invention would be useless. Therefore, one of his next inventions was the electric power plant. This is not a bad analogy to managing rental units, especially if you own a lot of them. The biggest limitation to your acquiring large numbers of rental units is the ability to handle the management of those units.

Most management companies charge 6% to manage your properties for you. Sometimes, single-family home management is up to 10%. If you decide to use a management company, you must include that cost when you estimate your cash flow.

All things considered, my recommendation is to start your company with self-management and periodically reevaluate as your business grows. The principle of starting small and growing with the business is a valid one. The ability to manage the business grows as the number of rental units increases.

There is nothing wrong with small beginnings. As you acquire new units, your confidence in your management skills will grow. When you begin to feel overwhelmed, slow down and reevaluate. Who knows, you may decide to start your own management company. Also, always remember that the banks, as well as other owners who may want to sell you their units and carry the loan, are watching to see how you perform. Do not take on more than you and your family can handle.

FAQ: What Professional People Do I Need?

Hire a good real estate broker.

Your first professional person to contact would be a real estate broker who specializes in investment property. Tell this person what you are looking for and let them do the legwork. Believe me, they will earn their commission as they scour the community for good deals. If an agent does not perform, then move on and go to another one. You want a mover and shaker working for you.

Your real estate agent can also recommend an inspection company from a list they have. Be sure to have the property inspected by a reputable company. This expenditure of $200 or so will pay large dividends. You want to guard against buying a house only to find out after the first big rain that the roof leaks and the basement floods.

Hire a good real estate attorney.

Your real estate broker can handle the contracts to a point, but as you get closer to making an offer and signing a contract, I recommend that you contact a good real estate attorney. Our failure to do this in the early stages of our career probably cost us more than we saved by not consulting an attorney.

A good attorney is essential to building a real estate investment business. They are not cheap, but if they keep you from making an expensive mistake, they will earn every dollar that you pay them. They may also help you avoid a costly lawsuit.

Hire a Good Certified Public Accountant.

As your business develops, you will need a good certified public accountant (CPA). Doing your taxes when investment real estate is involved is not possible unless you are an accountant with knowledge of depreciation schedules. Again, a good CPA can save you more that you pay them. A good accountant is costly but so are audits by the Internal Revenue Service. Do not make the mistake of tripping over dollars to pick up pennies.

Good professional people are well worth the fees they charge for their services. Fail to hire a good attorney and CPA at your own peril. I once told our CPA that when I received his bill, it seemed about half of what it should be. On the contrary, my attorney's bill seemed about double what I expected. A good CPA can save you money on your attorney bills by keeping you out of trouble.

FAQ: How Much Maintenance Should I Do?

Unless either you or your wife are handy, you will probably need a maintenance service. You may already have one that helps you on your home who would be happy for the extra work. Realtors sometimes have lists of handyman services and would be glad to recommend someone to you.

For major repairs, such as heating and air, we have usually called the service technician recommended by the seller of the particular unit. The same goes for appliances, unless it is something simple.

You will also need a cleaning service and painting contractor to assist you when the unit is vacated and re-leased. We did a lot of this maintenance ourselves in the early part of our career, but it is hard work and can quickly get old. You would probably be financially ahead to use a reputable professional in the first place.

Last, but not least, you will need the services of a good plumber. A good plumber is worth their weight in gold. I once tried to repair a toilet in one of our apartments. I made the problem worse and then called the plumber. Our plumber for the past 15 years once shared with me that the old adage that a stitch in time saves nine definitely applies to plumbing problems.

For Scripture says, "Do not muzzle an ox while it is treading out the grain," and "The worker deserves his wages" (1 Tim. 5:18).

Chapter 5

Taking the Next Step

Retirement From Teaching

Carol and I decided to retire from our teaching positions in May 1996. I told people that I needed to hire someone who could oversee my business, who would work cheap, and who I could trust, so I hired someone: me. Sam Jr. and I shared the responsibilities of managing the units while, at the same time, building the remaining ones.

After my Abraham moment on that starry night in August, I called my realtor friend that had sold me the lots for Sunset Place and asked if he had any other parcels that would accommodate one hundred units or so. I had discovered the economy of numbers. In order to have a manager and the amenities that we wished to put in our communities, I felt that we needed to build about one hundred units on one site.

Lazy hands make a man poor, but diligent hands bring wealth (Pr. 10:4).

Scenic Place Apartments

Our realtor friend had, just that day, received a listing on a six-acre tract just a couple of miles west of Sunset Place. I looked; I liked; I bought. We had managed to buy the ground for Sunset Place for 90¢ per foot, which was a bargain. We acquired the land for what would become Scenic Place Apartments for 36¢ per foot ($88,000). It was a steal by comparison.

One exciting aspect of this deal is that we had just sold the twelve-unit apartment building on East Cherry Street and were able to use the proceeds of that sale to purchase the land and serve as our input into this project. The density (units per acre) was lower, due to its location just outside the city. Even so, we built eighty-one units on the site and finished the project in August 1998.

Desiring to do something innovative, we built an indoor pool and hot tub. We also added three-bedroom units to our mix of one- and two-bedroom units. These three-bedroom apartments were some of the first built in our city.

The first building opened on July 1, 1997, contained eight one-bedroom units and eight two-bedroom units, and was fully leased. The second building, identical to the first, opened on August 1, 1997, and it too was fully leased. The third building was opened on September 1, 1997 and was also full.

The last three buildings, containing all three-bedroom units, were opened in March, May, and August 1998. Three students appreciated the ability to share expenses in a three-bedroom apartment, each having their own bedroom. The cost per student of these shared units was a modest $215 per month, plus electric, which they also shared.

The unit mix was twenty-four one-bedroom units, twenty-four two-bedroom units, and thirty-two three-bedroom units. We built a three-bedroom manager's unit over the office and clubhouse. Sam and Jennifer moved into this unit and were the first managers of Scenic Place Apartments. The clubhouse would later become a fitness center, and the manager's unit would become a rental unit for the rate of $820 per month.

When we had our grand opening, our old friend and mentor, Don Chadwick, was able to attend. He was particularly impressed with the indoor pool and hot tub.

Teach me, O Lord, to follow your decrees; then I will keep them to the end (Ps. 119:33).

Creative Financing

The construction of Sunset Place and Scenic Place Apartments was not easy. I frequently said that if our business were easy, more people would do it, and it would not be as profitable. On one occasion, we had to pay our plumber's bill ($30,000) by using several credit cards and paying them back over the next several months. We had sold our rental houses, the twelve-unit building, the eight-unit two-bedroom community, and the original ten-unit community that became fourteen when we built the four-unit building. We put all of the proceeds from these sales into these new properties.

We had also bought a rental house in Lompoc,

California. When we moved from Santa Barbara in 1986, Carol had wanted to keep our home there and turn it into a rental. I was not sure I wanted a rental that was located 1,700 miles away, so we sold the property. In hindsight, we should have refinanced the house and kept it. By 1988, the value of our small tract home in California had grown to $340,000, or about twice what we had sold it for just two years earlier.

Rather than regretting the selling of the Santa Barbara house, we moved up the coast and purchased a new home in Lompoc, California. A friend of ours, Pat Patterson, was looking for a nice rental and moved into the house as soon as it was finished.

We bought this house in 1989, and in 1993, were able to refinance the property and put the money ($25,000) into Sunset Place Apartments. We later sold the house to Pat and made $50,000 on the sale. This money also went into the financing of these two projects. The principle of starting small and growing was paying dividends. Once again, we learned the adage, "Despise not the day of small beginnings."

Dishonest money dwindles away, but he who gathers money little by little makes it grow (Pr. 13:11).

Aesthetics and Innovations: Art and Construction Merge

Carol and I had always believed strongly in curb appeal and aesthetics. We hired a decorator to help select the exterior colors, the brick, the interior colors, carpet, vinyl, appliances, windows, and floor plans. We also wanted our communities to have manicured landscaping, so we put irrigation systems in each of our communities. We put two baths in our two- and three-bedroom plans. We implemented innovations that we saw in new homes.

We tried to look into the future and imagine what apartments would look like in five or ten years. We built our floor plans with women in mind, realizing that there is at least one woman who influences the prospect's decision to lease or not. We also adhered to the saying that the three most important things in real estate are location, location, and location because, unless you are dealing in mobile homes, it is the one factor of real estate that cannot be changed.

Our locations had good visibility and excellent accessibility. We built near shopping, restaurants, and bus stops. We also chose locations that were in safe areas. My rule of thumb was if Carol and I could not walk the neighborhood after dark and feel safe, then we kept looking. Parents who are looking for a unit for their 18-year-old daughter who is attending one of the local universities have told me many times how much they appreciate the safety and security of our communities.

A builder once said, "Success is a thousand things done right." In multifamily building and management, we have found that to be true. Generally, we adhered to the idea that we would not own an apartment that we ourselves would not want to move into.

He will sit as a refiner and purifier of silver (Mal. 3:3).

The Village at Chesterfield:
The Dream Is Refined

Our next project was a condominium development in an area known as Chesterfield Village. We bought the land in order to construct an apartment community, but the developers decided they did not want any more high-density construction on their site so we built fourteen townhomes and eight patio homes instead and sold them. It was a beautiful project and is still one of the nicest condo developments in Springfield. We called this development "The Village at Chesterfield."

In the naming of all our developments, we used the name of the street on which they were located, if possible. Thus, Sunset Place was on Sunset Street. Scenic Place was near the corner of Scenic Avenue and Inman Road. In this way, a prospect could locate the community from the name of the apartment buildings.

As much as we enjoyed the Chesterfield Village project, the family agreed that our niche was still the apartment business. We were able to make some money on these units as we sold them. This capital would form part of the nest egg for our next project. We also refinanced both Sunset Place and Scenic Place and pulled some cash equity out of these projects to help us grow the company.

By this time, Daniel and David, our twin sons, had been hired and were managing Scenic Place. Our company now had several employees, and all but a couple were named Coryell. The condo project had taught us all a lot about where we wanted to be in our aesthetics and curb appeal as we looked into the future of our business.

May the Lord make you increase, both you and your children (Ps. 115:14).

Woodland Park Apartments: Sam Jr. and Jennifer Become Owners

We built our next apartment development on a parcel of land just east of Sunset Place. Don Chadwick had often said to me, "Sam, you should buy that land and build more apartments." I took his advice and we built Woodland Park Apartments, which consisted of sixty-eight one-bedroom units.

Sam Jr. and his wife, Jennifer, decided to be partners with us in this project. One nice thing about this development was that we were able to operate this community out of our Sunset Place office and use the same staff and pool and clubhouse. This project consisted of all one-bedroom units, and once again, it was full before we could get the buildings completed. The first building opened in March 2000, and the project was completed in August of that same year. Sam Jr. was the general contractor on this project.

I, wisdom, dwell together with prudence; I possess knowledge and discretion (Pr. 8:12).

Pinewood Park Apartments

As we were finishing Woodland Park, Paul White, our plumbing contractor, presented us with an opportunity to invest in a project in the community of Republic, Missouri. We liked the project and became partners with Paul in a ninety-seven-unit development that we named Pinewood Park Apartments. We did a unit mix of forty-eight one-bedroom units, forty-two two-bedroom units, and six three-bedroom units. An office, pool, and manager's unit completed the project. Sam Jr., Paul, and I built the project, which like Scenic Place and Woodland Park, was full by the time we opened the buildings.

Coryell, Coryell, and White, or CC&W, became the name of this new LLC. (We formed an LLC with each unique ownership group.) We would later sell this community, but we kept the partnership and would do another project with the proceeds from the sale of Pinewood Park Apartments.

For you, O Lord, are the Most High over all the earth; you are exalted far above all gods (Ps. 97:9).

Cambridge Park Apartments

We had purchased the Woodland Park land from Mr. Lee McLean, who also owned a parcel just down the block and across the street from Woodland. We bought this four-acre parcel and built Cambridge Park Apartments. We were also able to operate this community out of Sunset's office, but we decided to put in a pool at Cambridge. This project had eighty-six units.

The first building opened in July of 2001 and contained eight one-bedroom units and eight two-bedroom units. Four more identical buildings were built in a horseshoe shape with a six-unit building in the middle and a pool in front. The six-unit building contained four three-bedroom units and two one-bedroom units.

We would later build forty-eight units next door and put in an office and a workout facility. Cambridge Park eventually became 134 units and had a good mix of studios, as well as one-, two-, and three-bedroom units. Phase I was completed in late 2001 and Phase II in the spring of 2005.

By this time, Sam Jr. had become my right arm and began to move more and more into the construction side of the business. He and Jennifer moved to Scenic Place upon its completion to serve as managers at that location. Sam was majoring in construction management at Missouri State University and was an invaluable asset, both in the management and construction of the apartments.

The fear of the Lord is the beginning of wisdom; all who follow his precepts have good understanding (Ps. 111:10).

Jennifer: Salesperson Par Excellence

Jennifer was a born salesperson. Very effective in closing a deal, she engendered trust with everyone she met. Once I had shown a lady a one-bedroom unit, which overlooked the pool, and was surprised that she did not want to close the deal. She said she had some other appointments and would get back to me. I left her in the office with Jennifer and went to clean the pool.

When I returned about thirty minutes later, Jennifer informed me that the lady had signed the lease.

I asked, "What did you say to get her to close?"

She responded, "All I said was that I live here and that it is a wonderful place to live. I told her, 'You'll be sorry if you don't decide to live here.'" Jennifer was living in a one-bedroom at the time, and her sincerity and genuine love for her own Sunset Place unit enabled her to make the sale. I was, indeed, blessed with a capable staff.

In the late 1990s, a series of events occurred that propelled our business onto another plateau. Carol had discovered a small book entitled *The Prayer of Jabez* and gave each of us a copy for Christmas that year (2000). This book was based on a short passage in the book of I Chronicles:

Jabez was more honorable than his brothers. His mother had named him Jabez, saying, "I gave birth to him in pain." Jabez cried out to the God of Israel, "Oh, that you would bless me and enlarge my territory! Let your hand be with me, and keep me from harm so that I will be free from pain." And God granted his request (I Chron. 4:9–10).

We all enjoyed the book, but Jennifer, in particular, took it to heart. She and Sam Jr. began to pray daily that God would enlarge their territory. I believe that this concentrated prayer effort set us up for the next decade of growth in our business.

Also, at about the same time, Sam Jr. had established his construction company, Coryell Enterprises, Inc. This company would become the construction arm of TLC Properties.

The key to this rapid growth was our ability to hire good people to manage our properties. We found that people with a background in sales made good property managers. The key to having a successful real estate rental business is high occupancy, and good sales people keep your units full. These salespeople also had to be good administrators as well.

The other key to occupancy is taking care of the residents once they sign the lease. We found that one good person could manage about a hundred units. The larger communities required additional manpower such as a leasing agent. We found that new units could do well with one good maintenance man for every 250 units or so. We had the advantage in the beginning of being able to use family members. After we ran out of them, we interviewed people who answered our help wanted ads and using the above criteria, set out to hire the best that we could.

The banks, having seen that we knew what we were doing in the apartment business, would now allow us to build an entire project on one loan. We decided that, with Sam's company in place, we could build more than one project at a time by using different banks. We had constructed about 460 units by the end of 2001. Over the next seven years, we would build more than 2,500 units. During this time, we were able to open almost one unit per day!

FAQ: How Do I Determine
How Much Rent To Charge?

The best way to ascertain the rental rate for a particular area of a city is to do a market analysis of the rents in the area. Your friendly realtor can give guidance in this area, but this information can also be gained by checking the rents in the area yourself. The "For Rent" section in the classified ads is a good source. Simply call on a unit that is offered, which seems comparable to yours, and inquire about the price.

Another way to arrive at your asking price is to calculate how much the rental unit is costing you each month. If you have a mortgage, add your principle and interest payment, your insurance costs, and your property taxes (PITI). Add 25% for expenses, and that total amount should come close to representing your cost.

As an example, let us assume that your PITI is $500 per month. The 25% for expenses would amount to $125, which, when added to your mortgage payment, would yield a total monthly expense of $625. Using this formula, the lease rate should be somewhere between $650 and $695 per month. The actual price will depend on what the market will support. You do not want to be the most expensive nor the least expensive rental in the area. Somewhere in the middle of the market is a good place to set your rents.

One thing that we did early in our rental business career was to set the rent on the high side and then offer a discount of $25 per month if the tenant agreed to take care of minor maintenance. The exception to this was anything that had to do with water, such as a roof leak or a plumbing problem. (These were reported to the landlord without the tenants losing their discount of $25 per month.) The rent also had to be paid on time in order to receive the discount. If the rent was not paid by the 3rd of the month, the $25 discount was forfeited, and there was a $5 per day late fee that accumulated until the rent and late penalties were paid.

FAQ: What Is the Problem with Charging Low Rents?

One mistake that many new landlords make is setting their rents too low. Low rents invariably attract poor tenants. This pitfall occurs most often when the rental unit was inherited, and the only fixed expenses are the insurance and the taxes. In other words, there is no mortgage on the property. The new landlords get a false sense of their cost and set the rent at $500 when the market is actually $700 per month.

Usually, a first contact is made by telephone. The prospect has seen your sign in the yard or your classified ad and called to check on the rent. If you are charging $500 per month, the prospect may think, "If nothing goes wrong in our financial situation, we can just barely make that rental payment."

They decide to rent the house, and within a couple of months, something unexpected goes amiss in their financial picture (doesn't it always?), and the rent on your rental house is the first payment that your new tenants decide can wait awhile to be paid. The landlord in this situation becomes the tenant's banker because they now owe the owner $500 but are content to owe the money and allow the late fees to accumulate.

On the other hand, if you tell the prospect that the rent is $700, and they know that is out of their range, they will hang up the telephone. That is the least expensive eviction you will ever have.

Chapter 6

A Dream Is Fulfilled

You are good, and what you do is good; teach me your de-
crees (Ps. 119:68).

Lakewood Village Apartments

At the beginning of 2002, we were set up to build a lot of
units over the next several years. The first acquisition that we
needed to get our projects off the ground was the land on
which to build. The site must be in a good location, zoned for
multifamily development, and reasonably priced. We also
liked parcels that had high density so we could maximize our
investment. Sam Jr. found several parcels on the growing
southwest side of town. The sites were one block off a major
north-south artery on Lakewood Street.

The first acreage we purchased was the largest of the
available parcels. We decided to build three-story buildings
for the first time. We discovered that the more units we could
get under one roof and on one foundation, the better we was
able to maximize land use and thus maximize profits.

Another reason we opted for three-story buildings was that this development was a Planned Unit Development (PUD) and had a density of thirty units per acre. This marked one of the highest densities that we had been able to acquire.

To get all the parking we needed and have appropriate green space, we had to go up and build taller buildings. The lot was sloped and seemed perfect for a walkout basement. We decided to follow the natural contours of the land and build the buildings into the side of the slope.

Using the same configuration of our sixteen-unit buildings, we got eight more units by adding the third floor. This enabled us to construct twenty-four unit buildings on the same footprint as the sixteen-unit buildings. This approach also saved money due to our being able to get eight additional units on the same foundation and under the same roof. With the construction of every other building, in effect, we saved a foundation and a roof. This economy of numbers would guide us throughout the rapid expansion of our company over the next seven years.

We began construction on our first twenty-four unit building in January 2002 and completed it by June of that same year. Since we did not yet have an office, we used one of the one-bedroom units as our leasing office. This building contained twelve one-bedroom units and twelve three-bedroom units.

We were able to use similar floor plans to what we had done at our previous communities, with a few minor changes. The front of the building was two stories above ground, and the backside of the building was three stories. This configuration made the taller buildings less of a problem since one only had to go up or down one flight of stairs on the front side.

We used all our distinctive qualities that we learned to include in our apartments. We carefully selected the brick and siding colors. We had discovered that apartments look more like homes when they do not have facades that are all brick. The all-brick apartment communities could also look a little institutional if not done with the proper color of brick. Mixing in some siding gave a more balanced look to the project and saved money at the same time.

We overlapped the construction just as we had done in the past. Building C, the second building, opened in July 2002 and was similar to the first, except that we substituted two-bedroom units for the three-bedroom ones in building A. Building B was an office building that also had a one-bedroom unit and three studio apartments on the second floor.

These were the first studio apartments that we built. Our philosophy had always been to only build units that we would live in. Personally I did not like studio apartments, but we found that there was a niche for this type of unit in Springfield. So, we built these as a start into this unknown market.

Buildings D, E, and F were identical, in unit mix, to building C. Phase I of this project contained twelve three-bedroom units, sixty-one one-bedroom units, forty-eight two-bedroom units, and three studios for a total of 124 units. This was the largest community we had built to this point in our construction business.

Lakewood Village Apartments, like our other communities, had a pool and a hot tub. These amenities would also serve Phase II, which we completed in the spring of 2003.

These two buildings would contain 48 units, with one building having twelve three-bedroom units and twelve studio units and the other having twelve two-bedroom units and twelve one-bedroom units. Phases I and II contained 172 units when completed.

Rise up and help us; redeem us because of your unfailing love (Ps. 44:26).

Lakewood Trails Apartments

Sam Jr. and Jennifer had intended to build on a lot just across the street from Lakewood Village, but they discovered some problems with it. The seller had placed fill dirt into the steeply sloped site but had not prepared the fill in layers, as is required if one is going to build anything on the ground. Realizing the value of getting another sixty or so units in such close proximity to our existing units, I approached Sam Jr. with an idea.

I found out that the seller had already lost one sale to this problem and knew that he did not want to lose another. I suggested to Sam Jr. that we ask him to discount the lot in an amount commensurate with our added cost of removing the fill and replacing it in layers as required. He agreed, and we went forward with our plan.

The seller agreed to our price, and we began construction. We ended up getting fifty-eight units on the lot and called it Lakewood Trails Apartments because it had a city walking trail behind it. The units included forty-two one-bedroom units, ten two-bedroom units, and six studio units.

In the end there were a total of 230 units in these sister communities. Sam Jr. and Jennifer owned half of Lakewood Trails, while Carol and I owned the other half. Carol and I owned all of Lakewood Village Apartments. We were able to run both of these new units out of our Lakewood office.

We also built an amenity building that contained an activity center with weights and cardio equipment. This small building also had two tanning bed rooms and a large storage and work room under the activity center. The maintenance men referred to this work area as The Alamo because it looked like a fortress built into the side of a hill.

The construction of this large community set our company on a path to rapid growth. The principle of economy of numbers that we had learned was being put to use. We never would have been able to get this many units on these lots without our decision to build three-story buildings. This pattern of going vertical would continue over the next several years. Our next project would contain our first four-story building.

May the Lord make you increase, both you and your children (Ps. 115:14).

Sherwood Village Apartments

The name of Sherwood Village was one that I liked. On a visit to Baton Rouge, Louisiana, to see my brother, George, I passed Sherwood Middle School and thought that Sherwood would make a good name for an apartment community.

After we selected the name, we discovered that there was an elementary school of the same name about a mile away. Our usual policy (using a nearby street name or other local landmark in the naming of our communities) continued by accident.

The purchase of the land for Sherwood Village began with a call from a local real estate broker who wanted me to make an offer on Strawberry Fields Apartments. I was familiar with these apartments, which had been built in 1976. They were old, but there were about twenty-five acres of undeveloped ground surrounding these units. This property was on the corner of two major thoroughfares in the southwest area of Springfield.

Although I might not want the apartments, I knew that the land would be perfect for multifamily development and was already zoned for high density, which would give us the opportunity to build up to forty units per acre. This represented the highest unit density that we ever had in the past or would have going forward. Also, we would not have to go through the arduous process of getting the property rezoned.

I made an offer on the whole package that the owner turned down. I asked the realtor to inquire as to the owner's interest in selling the land apart from the apartments. The answer was in the affirmative so we bought the land on the north side of Strawberry Fields Apartments. The land, of course, was what we had wanted all along.

Marion Avenue dead-ended into these two lots: one on the east and one on the west. Sam Jr. and Jennifer decided to buy the west side, and Carol, Dan, Dave, and I bought the east side. We paid 90¢ per foot for the nine acres, which was zoned for high-density (forty units per acre) multifamily development.

The first building, which was supposed to be four stories tall, became a three-story building when we realized that we did not have enough parking. This property's location, which was within a couple miles of Missouri State University, would draw college students. Each one of them would have a car, and three students would share a three-bedroom unit. The city's requirement for parking for a three-bedroom unit was two spaces. We knew that our student tenants would need three spaces per three-bedroom unit. We chose to eliminate the fourth floor—eight units—to reduce our parking needs.

The first building opened in August 2003, which was just in time for the fall semester at the university. It contained 28 units that were a mix of three studios, seven one-bedroom units, twelve two-bedroom units, and six three-bedroom units. This building also had an office and storage room.

The second building opened in October 2003 and contained twelve three-bedroom units and twenty-four one-bedroom units. Building Three opened in January of 2004 and had twelve one-bedroom units, twelve two-bedroom units, and twelve three-bedroom units. All three of these buildings were three stories tall.

Building Four would be our first four-story construction. It contained 32 units, with two studios, ten one-bedroom units, fourteen two-bedroom units, and six three-bedroom units. The last building was another thirty-six unit and contained twelve studios and twenty-four two-bedroom units.

The total number of units at Sherwood Village Apartments was 168: seventeen studios, fifty-three one-bedrooms, sixty-two two-bedrooms, and thirty-six three-bedrooms. The amenities would include an indoor half-court basketball gym, an activity center that included a fitness center and pool table, a hot tub, and a swimming pool. We wanted our communities to have a resort feel.

May you be blessed by the Lord, the maker of heaven and earth (Ps. 115:15).

Sherwood Village East Apartments

In 2005, we had an opportunity to expand Sherwood by acquiring the land to the east. We purchased the corner, which included the land in front of Strawberry Fields Apartments that we had coveted for years.

Our plan was to get the back section of the highway frontage part of the commercially zoned property rezoned to multifamily and sell the remaining lots to commercial developers. Sherwood East became fifty-six additional units that used the amenities and management office of Sherwood Village. These two identical four-story buildings contained twenty-eight units, which had seven studios, seven one-bedroom units, and fourteen two-bedroom units apiece. These buildings opened in the summer of 2006.

The ability to construct fifty-six units and not have to add any personnel or amenities was a cost-saving idea that we had used before. This type of efficiency would become a hallmark of our development philosophy over the next several years.

O Lord, save us; O Lord, grant us success (Ps. 118:25).

Highland Park Apartments

At the same time that Dave, Dan, Carol, and I were building Sherwood, Sam Jr. and Jennifer, along with Jennifer's parents, Marty and Claudia Bess, were constructing Highland Park Apartments. In 2003, they opened their buildings: their first in April, their second in June, and their last in August. Highland Park contained eighteen two-bedroom units and seventy-eight one-bedroom units. They also put in a pool and office building with a one-bedroom manager's unit attached. Sam Jr. added covered parking to this community, and this amenity proved to be a popular one with the residents.

One scary event was a fire in February during the construction of the first building. Sam Jr. was out of town on business, and I was keeping an eye on his project. As I toured the building on a cold day in February, checking the propane heaters that were in use, one of the contractors came running and yelling, "Fire!" I ran upstairs, and to my horror, I discovered that my son's building was ablaze. We quickly called the fire department and formed a bucket brigade.

The fire trucks arrived within about five minutes and put the fire out. The fire-suppressant building practices that we had been using for years kept the fire in check until the firemen could get there. The fire was caused by one of the heaters falling over and catching the floor on fire. The lightweight concrete, or gyp-crete, which had been poured on the floor, worked to perfection and kept the fire contained. The damage was minimal, and the repairs were made without retarding the building schedule.

As iron sharpens iron, so one man sharpens another (Ps. 27:17).

Watermill Park Apartments

During the construction of Sherwood Village, I was asked to look at a site on the north side of town on Valley Watermill Road. The lot was in the county and had low density. It was also sloped similarly to Sherwood's site, and I was not sure that I wanted to build another project on a sloped lot.

I decided to pass on the site but received a call from a local builder who was interested in the location for himself. We met and talked, and as we parted, I said in passing, "If I can help you with your development, let me know."

A few months after this meeting, Jeff Boyce called and said that the bank insisted that he have a partner, and he wondered if I would be interested. Sam Jr. and I decided to take half of the project. We felt that it would be good for us to have a project on the north side of town. At this time, all of our communities were on the south side.

Jeff had been a homebuilder in the area and had built several nice houses. The project began in 2004 and was finished in about a year. The unit mix of the 164 units was fourteen studios, fifty-six one-bedrooms, fifty-six two-bedrooms, and thirty-eight three-bedroom units. We also built an office building with a workout center and a swimming pool. Just as the family had prayed in the prayer of Jabez, God was enabling us to enlarge our territory.

We would later buy out Boyce's interest. Sam Jr. and

Jennifer would own 45% of Watermill Park and Carol and I 55%. Having only one property on the north side proved to make it harder to use our network to assist in renting these units, but that situation was about to change as opportunities on the north side of Springfield began coming our way.

All those gathered here will know that it is not by sword or spear that the Lord saves; for the battle is the Lord's (1 Sa. 17:47).

Battlefield Park Apartments

As I drove west on Battlefield Road one afternoon, I saw a "For Sale" sign on a prime location. Although it was zoned for office use, I felt sure that we could get the property re-zoned for multifamily development.

The site contained two parcels of about five acres each. At first, the city agreed to rezone the back half but not the front. They felt that the highest, and best, use of the street frontage was office development. They would later change their mind after they saw what we had constructed on the back half of the property.

Each of the parcels were owned by different people, and because the city wanted a new street put in between the two properties, the buyer would have to make a deal with each owner. The city would not allow development of one lot without the other. We were able to acquire both parcels and began construction in 2004 after a long and arduous rezoning process. The first building, an eight-unit that consisted of all three-bedroom units, was finished in August of that year.

Phase I of Battlefield Park was completed in 2005 and contained 130 units: four four-bedroom units (our first of this type of unit), thirty three-bedroom units, forty-nine two-bedroom units, twenty-six one-bedroom units, and twenty-one studios. The city later allowed us to rezone the front section of the site because they liked the look of what we constructed on the back half. Phase I also contained the office, pool, and fitness center, which had two tanning beds. We also added four-bedroom units to our portfolio of apartments. These became attractive to students who could split the costs of the unit four ways.

The sluggard craves and gets nothing, but the desires of the diligent are fully satisfied (Pr. 13:4).

Battlefield Park, Phase II

After the city relented and allowed the rezoning of the entire site, we built Phase II and were able to add 112 additional units, which utilized the same office and amenities. We built two four-story buildings containing thirty-two units each and two three-story buildings containing twenty-four units each. The unit mix was twenty-eight studios, twenty-eight one-bedroom units, fifty two-bedroom units and six four-bedroom units. The two four-story buildings were on either side of the new street (South Sagamont) that we built through the center of the property.

Phase II of Battlefield Park Apartments opened in the spring and summer of 2006. Due to Battlefield Park's proximity to the university, we rented many of these units to students. Young coeds especially liked our large four-bedroom units.

Love your neighbor as yourself (Mt. 19:19b).

Good Neighbors

One of the big hurdles that we had to overcome in the construction of Battlefield Park was getting the multifamily zoning we needed. The site backed up to single-family homes on the south side. These homeowners had been flooded each time a heavy rain came through the area and had concerns about what our 242-unit development would do to the flooding problem that already existed.

Working with the city, we were able to alleviate this problem by putting in a large detention basin and an underground culvert that sent the run-off to a nearby sinkhole. The neighbors loved us. They never had any flooding issues again. We also put a privacy fence between our apartments and our neighbors to the south.

The city developers later confided in us that the culvert was needed before, but until we built our multifamily development, they could not justify the cost. Most of the time, our neighbors love our developments once they are finished. Any resistance in the beginning usually comes from a lack of knowledge and fears that the wrong kinds of people would be renting our units. When they saw the quality of our project and the type of residents that we attracted, they realized that our intent was to be a good neighbor.

Sam Jr. and Jennifer, along with her brother, Mike Bess, were partners on this project. This development became our largest one to date, with 242 units. This reaffirmed our belief that the more units we could get on one parcel of ground, the more cost-effective it was. The shared amenities and staff presented an economy of numbers that we had come to appreciate and seek out as our company continued to grow.

The construction of two four-story buildings opened our eyes to the value of building up to save money on the construction cost. Using less of our square footage of ground for apartment footprints allowed us more room for green space and parking. We had seen that each of the students in a four-bedroom unit would have a car. Although the city requirement for parking for that unit was only two, again we put in more parking than required because of our heavy student population.

When the righteous prosper, the city rejoices (Pr. 11:10b).

Plainview Park Apartments

A subcontractor of ours had some property on Plainview Road that he felt would make an ideal piece of land for a multifamily development. It was not bad, but it would have to be rezoned from commercial to residential multifamily. Sam Jr. and I, along with our wives, decided to join in partnership with Patrick Watkins and his attorney, Dan Nelson. Patrick had been our landscaper for several years and was excited to have the opportunity to work on a project with us.

Plainview Park construction began in early 2006 and was completed later that year. In addition to eighty-four apartments, we built an office, fitness center, and pool. We also added a tot yard because we knew that this part of town would attract families. The site was on the southwest side of town and felt somewhat secluded with trees on two sides. The setting had a country feel to it even though it was in the city.

The unit mix was split evenly between one- and two-bedroom units—forty-two of each. One of our regrets was our failure to build any three-bedroom units on this site. The site was small—only about three acres—and we were concerned about the parking requirements. Carol and I would later buy out Patrick and Dan's interests. Sometimes partners do not want to be in a development for the long run. We were happy for them to take their equity and do something else with it.

A greedy man stirs up dissension, but he who trusts in the Lord will prosper (Pr. 28:25).

Cedar Place Apartments

At about the same time that we built Plainview Park Apartments, we built Cedar Place Apartments in Republic, Missouri, which is a bedroom community just west of Springfield. This project was Sam Jr. and Jennifer's and proved to be expensive to build due mainly to its two-story construction. Since it was only 40 units, the economy of numbers that had applied to the larger projects did not work as well in this instance.

Cedar Place is a nice community, with a pool and exercise room, but it is difficult to support the costs and maintenance of these amenities in a 40-unit apartment community. The unit mix is one-, two-, and three-bedroom units. The primary appeal, other than local customers, is to those who enjoy living out of town. These residents will gladly drive a few miles to enjoy the quiet and serenity of suburban living.

He sought his God and worked wholeheartedly. And so he prospered (2 Ch. 31:21b).

FAQ: What Do You Do About Vacancies?

Paying mortgages on rental property only becomes a problem when they are not rented. Since vacancies can be a problem, add a little extra to the rent each month to help offset the cost of a vacancy. When a unit is vacated, put a sign in the yard, show the unit, and release the house.

Do not fear debt. About 95% of the world's wealth has been accumulated through real estate. This debt is enabled and supported by mortgages that are repaid by the tenants. Leverage can help you build a real estate empire, but you must first start your investing to reach your goals, whatever they might be.

FAQ: How Do I Screen My Prospects?

The easiest eviction you will ever have occurs when you say no to a prospect not financially qualified to afford the rent on your unit. It is legal to deny a person on the basis of their credit worthiness. Do a credit check and call their rental references. One good question to ask their previous landlord is, "If you had the chance, would you rent to this person again?" If their answer is no, then you should probably pass on the prospect.

One device that we used to help us determine a prospect's living habits was to walk them to their car and get a look inside. This had to be done without being obvious but could tell us a lot about how clean our rental unit would be after this person had lived there a year. If a prospect will not take care of a car, which they own, they will not take care of a house that they are only renting. Your rental unit will look like the back seat of their car at the end of their lease.

Chapter 7

Letting Go and Moving On

A Difficult but Necessary Decision

Carol and I had discussed selling Sunset Place on more than one occasion. Each time, I could tell that Carol was not yet ready to do so. In 2005, we decided to list the apartment community and see what kind of offers we could get. Our realtor produced a buyer at a reasonable price, and we decided to sell the ten-year-old property. The buyer also wanted to buy Woodland Park Apartments, which was adjacent to Sunset Place and use the same office and amenities.

Sunset Place was our first large development. For years afterward, each of our succeeding developments flowed from this development. Carol had an especially difficult time parting with this property, but we both knew that it was time. The new apartments that we were building seemed light years ahead of Sunset Place. We had learned so much over the past eleven years since we started this development, and we wanted to take our equity and build something on the southeast side of Springfield.

We kept our eyes and ears open for multifamily zoned

land on the southeast side of town but came up empty. As we were finishing up the contract on the sale of Sunset Place, my realtor mentioned that he heard that The Abbey was for sale.

The Abbey, which was located on 18 acres in the popular southeast area of town that we had searched but had been unable to find a suitable site, was only half completed. It had 165 units with a manager's unit. It was a beautiful project and only needed someone who could fill the units and complete the development. When completed, The Abbey would be one of the premier apartment communities in the city. We were bold enough to believe that we could do it.

In everything that he undertook in the service of God's temple and in obedience to the law and the commands, he sought his God and worked wholeheartedly. And so he prospered (2 Ch. 31:21).

We Purchase The Abbey

When Carol and I met with the owner and builder, Don Bracey, we were impressed with the construction of the apartments and the almost ten acres of land yet to be developed. The plan had been to build the community in a large oval shape, with five acres of green space and amenities in the center. Don had been unable to get the last building full, although it had been completed two years earlier.

Carol and I saw an opportunity to purchase The Abbey by using the proceeds from the sale of Sunset Place and Woodland Park. It was only through the sale of these two properties, containing 176 units, that we were able to purchase The Abbey. By using a 1031 like exchange, we traded our equity in these properties for the equity in The Abbey.

We also had to put $1,000,000 cash into the transaction. We had just refinanced Sherwood Village Apartments and had taken about that much in equity out of the property. The closing on the Sherwood loan occurred on November 6, 2005, and The Abbey purchase happened twelve days later. The total of the proceeds from the sale of Sunset Place and Woodland Park, plus the money from the refinance of Sherwood Village, was exactly the amount that we needed to close the deal with Don Bracey and his partners.

It shone with the glory of God, and its brilliance was like that of a very precious jewel (Rev. 21:11a).

We Have a Jewel

I moved my manager, Michael, from Sunset-Woodland to The Abbey. The former manager of the property decided to move on to another position. "Michael," I said on that first day of ownership, "we have a gem, but it will take some polishing to get where we need it to be." He agreed, and we hired a decorator, John Greenhall, to help us spruce up the place.

One staff holdover, Dena the assistant manager, was in charge of the so-called corporate rentals. These units were fully furnished like hotel rooms. She informed me on my first day of ownership that all a person needed to move into one of these units was their clothes and a toothbrush. She also told me that there were twenty-three unfurnished units that sat vacant.

I asked Dena to tell me about these corporate units because we had only one in our entire network until we bought The Abbey. Dena informed me that we had twenty-five total of these types of units and added, "They stay rented almost all the time. We rarely have a vacancy for more than a few days."

I said, "Why don't we turn some of these twenty-three unfurnished units that are vacant into corporates?"

She responded, "You furnish them, and I will rent them."

We did furnish them, but it took an expenditure of capital to make it happen. Michael and I scouted for the best quality furniture for the money, and we slowly began to put our new corporate units together. Michael had a gift for decorating and loved to spend my money. About $100,000 later, we had twenty additional corporates.

In April 2006, the Springfield Cardinals' players came to town, looking for living quarters. Our new corporates were just what they and their managers were looking for. On April 6, 2006, Michael called me and said, "Sam, The Abbey is fully rented." I congratulated him on a job well done.

For surely, O Lord, you bless the righteous; you surround them with your favor as with a shield (Ps. 5:12).

Filling Up The Abbey

Don Bracey, the original owner and builder of The Abbey, had commented once that he felt our company was the perfect one to complete The Abbey. When I asked him why he felt that, he said, "Because the bank will not loan me the money to complete it until I fill the existing units. I believe that your company, with your large network, can accomplish that and get the rest of the development built." I could not have agreed with him more.

Our network had grown exponentially over the past several years. When a prospect walked into one of our offices, in effect, they were visiting our entire network. We had trained our managers and assistants to work the network if they did not have exactly what the prospective resident needed.

We began working hard at branding the TLC Property name in the community. Our goal was to have everyone in our demographic aware of our global company, TLC Properties. This network advantage, in addition to the addition of the twenty corporates, enabled us to get our occupancy to 100% at The Abbey.

A little luck did not hurt, either. The Springfield Cardinals' decision to send their players and managers to The Abbey put us over the top. It is said that successful people make their luck. We had prepared for the Cardinals coming, even though we did not know we would have the opportunity to rent units to them. We also contacted companies in our area and acquainted them with our new corporate units. One of the calls we made was to the Springfield Cardinals.

Faith without deeds is dead (Jas. 2:26).

When we purchased The Abbey, there was a unit in the C wing that had been vacant for more than two years. It was a 1,650 square foot two-bedroom unit that rented for $1,200 per month. The previous owners had lost over $28,000 on this one unit during the past twenty-four months.

We were determined not to let that loss of income continue. We turned it into a corporate unit and rented it in about five minutes to the first person we showed it to. Michael had done a masterful job of decorating this beautiful unit, and we kept the price at $1,200, even though the apartment was now completely furnished. The adage, "Doing the same thing and expecting different results is one definition of insanity," is true. We had made all the necessary changes and so we had a right to expect a different result.

Completing The Abbey

By the summer of 2007, we were able to get all of the permits and financing in place to enable us to begin construction on the remainder of The Abbey. The only aspect of the original Abbey that I did not like was the use of galley kitchens in most of the units. In the new Abbey, we opened up the kitchens and put in a bar. This one change modernized the units and gave the illusion of more space. These open floor plans appealed to our women residents.

We also chose exciting decors that people (especially women) seemed to like. The original Abbey had elevators, and we continued this amenity in the new section. The Abbey had been thought of as a 55 and older community, although it was not. Michael and his staff did a good job of changing people's view of The Abbey. We began to attract young people and even a few students. The young women liked our new and improved kitchens.

The original Abbey had a clubhouse in the middle of the five-acre courtyard that was almost never used. We turned it into a fitness center with weights and cardio equipment and a game room with a pool table and a ping-pong table. The facility also had a kitchen that the residents could use for parties and other special occasions. We added a putting green and a tot yard to the existing outdoor amenities of tennis and basketball courts and a sand volleyball court. We also added an athletic pool to the existing pool and hot tub.

The crowning amenity at The Abbey was a movie theater on the third floor that could seat up to thirty-three people. Every Friday and Saturday evening, we show a movie at 6:30 and 8:30, and we furnish the popcorn. The theater is also used for special occasions, such as Super Bowl Sunday, March Madness, and the World Series. Residents can reserve the theater, if they desire, for a modest fee.

The resort atmosphere that we had been moving toward for the past few years became a reality at The Abbey. For five years (2008 through 2012), The Abbey was chosen as the Best Multifamily Community of the Year by the readers of the *Springfield News-Leader* in their annual publication of Best of The Ozarks. During this same five-year span, TLC Properties was selected as the Best Property Management Company by the *News-Leader*.

Those who are wise will shine like the brightness of the heavens (Da. 12:3a).

Three-Bedroom Units with Three Baths

We added seven three-bedroom units to the mix in the new Abbey. The original Abbey contained seventy-six one-bedroom units, seventy-four two-bedroom units, and sixteen studios. The new Abbey would have fourteen studios, seventy-two one-bedroom units, and seventy-two two-bedrooms, in addition to the spacious three-bedroom units mentioned above. Four of the three-bedroom units had three full baths. These units were in excess of 1,650 square feet of living space. All of the third floor units in the new Abbey had eleven-foot ceilings. These units gave the illusion of more living space because of the increased cubic space due to the tall ceilings. Since we built elevators in these buildings, the third-floor units were the most popular, and we charged more rent for them.

The eighth, and final, wing of The Abbey was completed in January 2009. After trying several sources but failing to get our permanent financing on this project, we applied for a HUD loan in July 2010. The loan closed on November 30, 2011, and amortized over thirty-five years at an interest rate of 4.4%. We were thrilled to get this loan, but getting it was like going to your dentist for a root canal and having the procedure without any anesthetic.

The HUD inspectors commented that The Abbey was one of the most impressive developments that they had ever inspected. I wondered how long a project that the inspectors did not find appealing would have to wait to get their financing.

You will keep in perfect peace him whose mind is steadfast, because he trusts in you (Isa. 26:3).

Bradford Place Office Condominiums

In early 2006, we sold Scenic Place Apartments to a group of investors from Florida. Since we did not want to pay the capital gains taxes due on this sale, we did a 1031 like property exchange. We had designated three properties in our proclamation, but two of the properties did not work out. The only one that did was the office building where we leased the TLC Properties corporate offices. Although we owned no office buildings at the time, we bought the second and third floors of the beautiful building and moved our growing business into a prime spot on the third floor.

This building, Bradford Place, is one of the few class-A office properties in Springfield. Consequently, the rents are on the high side, and the larger offices proved a challenge to maintain when the economy collapsed in the fall of 2008. The smaller offices proved easy to re-lease when they came open, but it has been difficult to keep the rents high enough to support the mortgage and maintenance costs. At full occupancy, we make money, but with a vacancy of one of the large units, we do not. As a result, we occasionally have to capitalize the building. We decided that we should stick to our niche of apartments.

So they built and prospered (2 Ch. 14:7c).

FAQ: How Do I Know When To Sell a Property?

In our experience at TLC Properties, the time to sell has been obvious. As builders, it makes a lot of sense to sell an older property and invest the proceeds from the sale in a new and better property. If you have partners, it is sometimes difficult to agree on selling and taking your profit or refinancing and holding. Each will yield some capital, but there are times when refinancing is better than selling due to capital gains taxes that will no doubt be due on the sale of a rental property.

Sometimes it becomes difficult to sell because of emotional attachments to a property. It was difficult to sell our first large property, Sunset Place Apartments. We had owned it for eleven years, and everything that we had done since we built it had flowed from that property. When we had an opportunity to buy a prime piece of real estate on the southeast side of town, however, we knew that it was time to sell.

We did a 1031 like exchange, thereby deferring the capital gains taxes on the sale. This type of exchange has very strict rules and must be handled with the advice of a good real estate attorney but can save the buyer thousands of dollars in capital gains taxes.

We have done several of these exchanges and have found them to be an excellent way to buy units and avoid the biggest reason not to sell: capital gains taxes. Remember, the tax is deferred, not canceled. Either the owner or his heirs will pay the tax in the future when the property sells.

FAQ: How Do I Determine the Value of a Property?

The value of investment real estate is determined by the income that the property produces. In an appraisal, there are three types of values: the cost approach, comparable sales in the area, and the income approach. The income approach is the preferred type for income producing property.

There is a simple formula that is used for rental property that is known as the "IRV" formula. The "I" represents income, the "R" is the cap rate for the area, and the "V" is for value. In this calculation, value equals the income divided by the cap rate. A local appraiser, banker, or real estate broker can provide a range of cap rates on rental houses in the city. This rate varies depending on various economic conditions. Suffice it to say that if you are buying, you want a high cap rate. If you are selling or refinancing, you want a low cap rate.

Let us use the example of the rental house in an earlier example that leased for $650 per month. The annual income would be 12 times $650 or $7,800. You then subtract 25% for expenses and arrive at an annual income of $5,850. Assuming a 7.5% cap rate for the area, the value of this rental house is $78,000. The higher you can push the rent, the higher the value. A modest increase in the rent to $700 over a couple of years would yield an increased value in the house of $6,000. This increase in value becomes important when you sell or refinance the property.

Chapter 8

More Construction

Hawthorn Suites Apartments

In 2006, Sam Jr. and Jennifer purchased Hawthorn Suites Apartments located in the popular southeast part of town. Again, like The Abbey, Hawthorn's appeal was that it had about four acres to develop, and it was located next door to the YMCA, which had an indoor pool, basketball courts, racketball courts, and a large workout gym. Sam was able to make a deal with the YMCA—for a fee, included in the cost of their rent, his residents could use the beautiful facilities.

Later that year, Sam Jr. began construction on three 32-unit buildings to add to the existing four 8-unit buildings. Finished in 2008, Hawthorn Suites has 128 units with an even mix of one-, two-, and three-bedroom units. The location near the James River Freeway allows our company, TLC Properties, to have fantastic advertising on the sides of the buildings through attractive neon signs. Everyone in town knows where that property is located and that it is a TLC managed property.

Sam Jr. secured a HUD loan on this project in September of 2009. The 35-year amortization schedule and the low interest rate will enable this property to keep its debt cost low for the next three and a half decades. With this attractive loan, Hawthorn Suites Apartments will be able to compete well as interest rates rise over the next several years.

My son, do not forget my teaching, but keep my commands in your heart, for they will prolong your life many years and bring you prosperity (Pr. 3:1–2).

Martin Riley Apartments

My favorite aspect of this apartment community is its name. Martin is the middle name of my grandson, Samuel, and Riley is the middle name of my granddaughter, Lydia. Riley was also my mother's maiden name.

This project embodied the concept of the "big house." Although the units look like several big houses, they are actually apartment units. It is a beautiful project on the southeast side of Springfield, and like Hawthorn Suites, it is near a freeway and has excellent visibility.

Sam put in some nice combination storage units and covered parking as an amenity for the residents. The property also has a pool and workout room. Once again, the economy of numbers made this a difficult project due to its size—58 units—and its cost. It is a lovely community, and although the single-family homeowners in the neighborhood objected to the rezoning of this land to multifamily, they loved the finished product.

Sam and Jennifer sold this community in the spring of 2012. After six years, they decided to take their equity and invest in a new and larger project in the southeast part of town.

He who pursues righteousness and love finds life, prosperity and honor (Pr. 21:21).

Marion Park Apartments

In 2005, the family decided to purchase the acreage in front of Strawberry Fields and build apartments on the back half of the property. We would leave the front half commercially zoned but get the back lots rezoned to high-density multifamily. This process took time due to the city's requirements of a street and other infrastructure, which included a signal on the major street in front of the property.

We began construction in 2006 and finished near the end of 2007. We wanted to do something different in this project, and we made the floor plans bigger than our "bread and butter" units. The prospective residents loved the space but did not want to pay the higher rental rates that these larger units demanded.

These 128 units were in a four-story walkup, and the units on the fourth story had vaulted ceilings. This amenity became necessary as we built taller buildings in order to entice people to go up three flights of stairs. When these units first opened, we charged more rent for the fourth floor units because of the increased cubic feet of space. The unit mix— thirty-two studios, forty one-bedroom units, forty two-bedroom units, and sixteen three-bedroom units—worked well with those of Sherwood Village and Highland Park that were located just to the north.

The amenities included a pool, fitness center, and a 30-seat movie theater. We later added shuttle service to Missouri State University, since over half of our residents were college students. This shuttle service also served our other properties on this corner. The ownership of Marion Park included our three sons, Sam, Dan, and Dave; Carol's sister and brother-in-law, Liz and Jim Miller; Jennifer's brother and his wife, Mike and Renee Bess; Jennifer's father and mother, Marty and Claudia Bess; and Carol and myself.

He who gets wisdom loves his own soul; he who cherishes understanding prospers (Pr. 19:8).

Orchard Park Apartments

In 2005, Sam Jr., Paul White, and I decided to purchase twenty acres on the northwest side of town and build a large community together. This proved to be a difficult project due to various infrastructure issues, but we began construction in 2006. Phase I—256 units—was finished in the summer of 2007. My brother, George Coryell, had come to Springfield to be a part of another project down the road and became our first manager of this large project.

Phase I had eight buildings with thirty-two units each. The eight buildings contained sixty-four studios, sixty-four one-bedroom units, sixty-four two-bedroom units, forty-eight three-bedroom units, and eight four-bedroom units.

The community also had a large pool, a kiddie pool, a smoothie and coffee bar, a recreation room, a fitness center, and a 72-seat movie theater. We would later add tennis and basketball courts as well as dog parks in the Phase II section of the development.

Orchard Park was located on the I-44 freeway with great visibility and easy accessibility. It was also located just across the street from T-Mobile, a call center for the mobile phone company. The employees of our neighborhood could walk to work if they lived in our community.

George did a terrific job of leasing the Phase I portion of Orchard Park. When he left to go to the project he was originally part of, the property was full. Because of the ease of the rapid rent-up of the first buildings, we decided to go forward with the second phase. What we did not count on was a massive downturn in the economy. We thought that all we had to do was build our apartments, and the residents would flock to our doors. The recession of late 2008 changed everything, and we did not see it coming.

Although there was some trepidation about building Phase II of Orchard Park, the speed at which George was able to lease the 256 units encouraged us to continue. We found a bank that gladly loaned us the money to complete the project and began construction in early 2008. Everything seemed to go well until the fall of that year when the economy took a drastic downturn.

Orchard Park, located near the Springfield-Branson Regional Airport and the Springfield Industrial Park, attracted many blue-collar workers. The great recession forced many of these residents out of work, and they could no longer afford their apartments. They moved in with Mom and Dad or with friends, leaving us with vacant apartments. The new apartments in Phase II rented well, but we began to suffer vacancies in the Phase I section.

We wisely decided to cap Phase II at 160 units instead of the planned 304 units. We still plan to build 144 more units when the economy will allow it. Phase II included twenty-four studios, forty one-bedroom units, fifty-six two-bedroom units, thirty-two three-bedroom units, and eight four-bedroom units. We added tennis and basketball courts and additional picnic areas to the existing amenities. We used the office and amenities of Phase I for these units.

Like our other properties, whose construction ended after the great recession began, we could not obtain permanent financing on Phase II of Orchard Park, although we tried valiantly to do so. We finally opted to get a HUD loan on the entire property. The bank that held the mortgage on Phase I wanted to get rid of the loan and offered us a discount if we could find a bank to take over the loan. Wanting to take advantage of this offer, nonetheless, we failed to procure the HUD loan before another bank took the discount.

Sam Jr. negotiated with the new bank and finally talked them into passing part of the discount that they had received on to us so that we could close our HUD loan. The bank that held the loan on Phase II agreed to follow the first bank's lead. Both banks agreed to a discount that totaled $640,000, but there was one catch—we had to close on the HUD loan no later than March 1, 2012.

Through much prayer and many nervous days, we closed the HUD loan on Orchard Park Apartments on February 28.

The closing, however, was late in the day, and the payoffs to both banks were not made until the next day, February 29, 2012. Thank God for leap year! We refer to this as our miracle closing. The owners, Sam Jr. and Jennifer, Daniel, Carol, and I agreed that every February 29, we would have a special time of thanksgiving for this provision in our professional lives. Each time I think of this closing miracle, I say a prayer of thanksgiving for God's leap year blessing.

He sought his God and worked wholeheartedly. And so he prospered (2 Ch. 31:21b).

Palm Village Apartments

The Lord will grant you abundant prosperity (Dt. 28:11a).

As we surveyed areas for building apartments, we always first looked in areas where we already had units. I had long wondered about a lot that was located just across the street from Cambridge Park Apartments. David and Daniel decided to purchase this three-acre parcel and construct as many units as they could.

The lot was zoned for office buildings and priced at $4 per foot. The total cost would be over $600,000. This was on the high side for multifamily, which made it necessary to put as many units on the parcel as possible.

Because of the property's zoning, we had to go through the rezoning process. We began construction in 2006 and opened the first building in June 2007. David became the construction manager and showed an interest and passion for the process that impressed me. He has champagne taste, and consequently, his wonderful ideas cost money. The finished product, Palm Village Apartments, looked as though it belonged in Palm Springs. The landscaping included palm trees (artificial), and the façade was all stucco. It became one of our most beautiful communities.

The amenities for the 83 units included a pool and workout facility. All three of the buildings—a sixteen unit, a thirty-two unit, and a thirty-five unit—were four-stories tall. The sixteen unit housed all four-bedroom units, which again proved popular with the university students who shared expenses. Fifteen of the sixteen units were leased before the building opened.

The additional 67 units included nineteen studios, sixteen one-bedroom units, sixteen two-bedroom units, and sixteen three-bedroom units. The community was completed by the end of the summer of 2007. The close proximity to our existing property across the street allowed us to use that office to prelease the Palm Village units before the office was completed. Since its completion, the friendly relationship with the sister community, Cambridge Park, has allowed our company to interchange staff in emergency situations over the past five years.

David and Daniel's original partners on this project wanted to sell out earlier in 2012. Carol and I eagerly stepped in to become owners of this lovely property. After all, we do have a long-standing relationship with the remaining owners—our sons.

Since becoming partners, we have been able to refinance the property and lower our interest rate. David, who enjoys this aspect of our business, led the way in this refinance as well as others.

Blessed are all who fear the Lord, who walk in his ways. You will eat the fruit of your labor; blessings and prosperity will be yours (Ps. 128:1–2).

Coryell Crossing Apartments

In 2005, we did a feasibility study on building a tower apartment community to the east of Marion Park Apartments. The extra costs involved in the concrete and steel construction required in a building over four floors seemed daunting, but we decided to go ahead and hire the architects to draw the plans. This building would be twelve stories tall.

After a year of working on this project, we decided to go back to conventional four-story construction due to increased costs of steel and concrete construction. With the four 32-unit buildings and the one 48-unit building we put on the site, we got more units than we would have with the tower.

The first building at Coryell Crossing opened in March of 2007. A building followed about every six weeks, and the community was completed in the fall of 2007. We also built an office with a fitness center and recreation room.

One new feature of Coryell Crossing included a forty-eight unit building. It was to have been a sixty-four unit building, but we had concerns about parking and reduced the building by twelve units. The unit mix became forty studios, forty-one one-bedroom units, forty-seven two-bedroom units, twenty-four three-bedroom units, and twenty-four four-bedroom units. We put in an athletic pool, which meant that there was the potential to play pool volleyball, and that proved to be a popular addition.

We had sold the street side lots to a commercial developer who put in a strip center that leased to businesses appealing to apartment dwellers. A popular restaurant, The Roost, which specialized in chicken wings; a tanning salon; and other stores that appealed to our clientele of 1,500 residents, were all within easy walking distance.

The new street that we put in was named University Street, which seemed appropriate since students represented over half of our residents at this location. We also ran a shuttle service for the students that took them to and from school. The university liked this service too because our shuttle removed cars from their crowded campus. This service also allowed us to compete with rental units adjacent to the university.

We took Coryell Crossing's name from a ferry crossing that my brother George learned of. He loaned the property a painting of this ferry, called Coryell Crossing, that we hung in the leasing office. (I also liked the alliteration.)

Do not let this Book of the Law depart from your mouth; meditate on it day and night, so that you may be careful to do everything written in it. Then you will be prosperous and successful (Jos. 1:8).

Coryell Courts Apartments

As we continually looked for good opportunities to expand our business, I saw a beautiful lot for sale overlooking the I-65 corridor on the northeast side of Springfield. The acreage had once been a driving range and miniature golf course. The site was zoned for industry and would need to be rezoned for multifamily development. I approached the City Planning Department, and they encouraged me to apply. A few months later and $1,000 poorer, the city zoning committee decided not to support our application for the rezoning.

I kept looking and drove to a site on the north side of Springfield located near the I-44 corridor. The visibility and accessibility of this parcel did not meet our criteria, but as I drove to turn around on the dead-end street, I spotted a "For Sale" sign for acreage that had great visibility from I-44 and easy access.

Another attractive aspect of this site was the fact that it was already appropriately zoned for apartments. The density was thirty units per acre, which would allow us to construct 400 units on the 14.11 acres. We decided to buy the land and began the process of getting our permits to build what would become Coryell Courts Apartments.

The owners of this new community would be the family: Sam Jr., Jennifer, Daniel, David, Carol, and I, plus my brother George and his wife, Sheryl. The partners all brought their unique talents to this large project. David insisted that we go first class, as long as it did not bust our budget. Sam Jr. and his construction company, Coryell Enterprises, managed the job site and worked with the architects. Carol, Jennifer, and

Sheryl added the woman's touch and had many good ideas about the floor plans. Daniel helped me in the general oversight of the project, and George helped us from the marketing side of the business, as well as bringing ideas about amenities and floor plans.

One important suggestion that George made was to put a nice metal fence on the front and east side of our community. (We had already built a privacy fence on the back and west sides of the project.)

The completion of Coryell Courts, like most of our projects, proved to be a team effort. Fortunately, the team members seldom disagreed on the big things. I do recall one situation where David and I did not see eye-to-eye. We were trying to finish the office building, but the black bathroom stall dividers were on back order. I suggested that we put in beige dividers, but David insisted that we wait. I reluctantly waited, and I am happy to say that David was right. The bathrooms at Coryell Courts' office are beautiful, and the black divider stalls do make a difference.

Due to the necessity of putting in a half-acre water detention basis, we lost forty units, but 360 units would make this community our second largest.

We wanted to do something a little different with this project. We hired an architect, Steve Busch from Tulsa, Oklahoma, to design our buildings. Again, we wanted our new community to feel like a resort, so we put in the usual amenities: pool, hot tub, and fitness center, along with tanning beds. We also added a large movie theater to the office building.

Building A opened in December of 2007. My brother,

George, became the manager. He had managed Orchard Park Apartments and successfully filled the first phase, which consisted of 256 units. We knew that he would take ownership because he had a 20% interest in the project.

George sold cars in Baton Rouge, Louisiana, for several years and, like Jennifer, could sell ice to Eskimos. He had a charm and wit that enabled him to find common ground with prospective residents. He developed a friendship with the members of his community, and he became our best closer, setting a high standard for our other managers.

Building A of Coryell Courts contained forty units. Each of the five buildings in Phase I would have a good mix of studios, and one-, two-, and three- bedroom units. Phase I construction wrapped up in August 2008 and consisted of 200 units and a large amenity building. George did a great job of filling these units. The finished units became a big hit on the north side of town. The Steve Busch-designed buildings looked unlike any apartments in our city. They had a French country style that appealed to our clientele.

We began Phase II in 2008 and finished the project in October 2009. We decided to put elevators and internal hallways in this phase. We added a security entrance where the resident must buzz in the visitor. We also added every type of game requiring a court that we could. I liked the sound of Coryell Courts, but I also wanted the name to reflect the property. The courts we put in included basketball, tennis, and shuffleboard. We also added a tot yard and green areas with grills and picnic tables for barbeques.

Phase II would also contain a new floor plan: The Sam Sr. As we thought about the design of the new phase, we asked George if we needed to change anything from Phase I. He said that he felt the additional three-bedroom units might become more difficult to rent. We decided to take sixteen of the three-bedroom footprints and construct sixteen large two-bedroom units instead. These new units proved to be popular due to the master bath and walk-in closet, which were both quite large. The large master bedroom also had a built-in desk.

These 160 units included thirty-two studios, forty-eight one-bedroom units, sixty-four two-bedroom units, and sixteen three-bedroom units. The first 200 units contained forty studios, sixty one-bedrooms, sixty two-bedrooms, and forty three-bedrooms.

When we could not find permanent financing for Coryell Courts during the recession, we decided to apply for a HUD loan. When one of the HUD inspectors came to our community to check our units, he commented to me that Coryell Courts was one of the nicest projects that he had ever inspected. I could not agree more with the HUD inspector's assessment. Coryell Courts Apartments is a beautiful community, and I am proud of our company's accomplishment.

After two years, we closed our HUD loan on Coryell Courts on June 22, 2012. Our interest rate of 4.1% amortized over thirty-five years was a blessing that will keep on giving over the next three decades and more. The tasks of acquiring one of these loans is arduous but well worth the time and effort once they are in place.

Coryell Courts marked the fourth HUD loan that we had acquired on our properties. The other three properties were

Hawthorn Suites, The Abbey, and Orchard Park Apartments. With the low interest loans and the thirty-five year amortizations that are in place, these properties will be well positioned over the next three decades to compete in the marketplace due to the fact that the debt service will remain the same for three-and-a-half decades. Our goal is to get more of our larger properties, that we intend to keep, on these types of long-term loans.

> *If they obey and serve him, they will spend the rest of their days in prosperity and their years in contentment* (Job 36:11).

FAQ: How Do I Deal With Evictions?

This is the area of our business that can be the most discouraging to a new landlord. Tenants who were late on their rent have said to me, "You don't need my money. You have all these units. You are rich." The fact that they signed a contract and agreed to pay me for the use of my rental property becomes irrelevant to them. At this point, the wise landlord just wants to get the unit back and lease it to someone that pays the rent. The sooner you can get this accomplished, the better it will be for your property and your wallet.

In these situations, the landlord has two choices: actual eviction or peaceful eviction. Actual eviction requires a court action, and if you are operating your business as a Limited Liability Corporation, you will require an attorney. The cost will be in the $300 range, and you will get your unit back in about a month.

The peaceful eviction involves negotiating with the tenant and arriving at a mutually beneficial arrangement. I have told delinquent tenants that if they will move by the 15th of the month and have the unit cleaned, I will give them back a portion of their deposit. You are paying them to move out in order to save the greater cost and lengthier process of an actual eviction.

The danger for the landlord, in the peaceful eviction, is that if the tenant fails to move out, the owner must then start the legal process two weeks later. Sometimes, the tenant is stalling and has no intention of moving. Nonetheless, we almost always try the peaceful eviction first before we proceed to the actual eviction and go to court.

Whichever eviction process you decide to use, act

quickly. The resident will try to buy time, but just know that you are going to lose money on this deal. You must stop your losses as quickly as possible and move on. Trying to redeem the situation and work with the tenant on a payment plan almost never works. All that happens is that the tenant gets to live in your unit rent-free for a few more days, weeks, or months. Act fast to limit your losses.

The simplest eviction you will ever have is the one that does not happen because you did your due diligence on the front end and said no to a prospect that you felt uneasy about. Screening prospects is a little like dating—ignore the red flags at your peril.

Most real estate investment people are trusting and would, in the beginning, never believe that a tenant would purposely lie. However, there are people who pride themselves on living almost rent-free. In a continuing education class I took some years ago, a realtor told of such a tenant. The con man had boasted that he only paid his rent about two or three months out of the year. The realtor explained that the tenant said that he simply paid his deposit and first month's rent with a bad check. By the time the owner's bank notified the landlord of the insufficient funds and the tenant was evicted, he had lived in the house or apartment rent-free for several months.

In your screening process, check with your local apartment association for any and all lists they might have that serve to warn unsuspecting landlords of freeloaders. Many communities have a local affiliate of the National Apartment Association (NAA). The sixty realtors who attended this class on property management could not believe that such practices occur. There are con artists who will take advantage of their landlord. Do not allow such people to succeed in scamming your community. Do your due diligence and force these miscreants to pay their own way.

FAQ: Should I Allow Pets in My Rental Units?

This question can become one of the toughest decisions a landlord must make. Early in our business, we decided to accept pets with a weight limit of 25 pounds. We also instituted a pet fee of $200 that was not refundable. We found, however, that these steps alone did not keep tenants and their pets from inflicting expensive damages on our rental units.

We later insisted that the prospect provide evidence from their veterinarian that the pet had been spayed or neutered. Male cats left un-neutered will spray the carpet, and that is an odor that is difficult, if not impossible, to remove.

Another problem we encountered was the "illegal" pet. This is a pet that has not been approved by management. After replacing several carpets that had been ruined by illegal pets, we put harsh fines into our lease for having pets that we did not approve. Collecting such fines proved difficult, but it is still worthwhile to have them in place in case of legal action. Even if one fails to collect damages, there will still be a judgment against the tenant. Again, consult your attorney on how one might pursue cases such as these.

Today, TLC Properties requires renter's insurance. Each resident must purchase a renter's policy in order to protect us from having to either pay for damages out of our pocket or pay an expensive deductible to have our insurance pay. A carpet that has to be replaced can consume one year's profit or more on a single rental unit. Requiring renter's insurance is one way to prevent these types of expensive losses from occurring.

One side note that I will add involves a positive aspect of allowing pets. A few years ago, at Cambridge Park Apartments, one of our managers, Les Butterfield, was awakened at 3:00 a.m. by his dog. When he got out of his warm bed to see what disturbed his pet, he saw flickering lights out of his bedroom window. As he looked to see what this was, to his horror, the building next to his was on fire. The flames on the deck just across from his apartment were already lapping at the eaves and threatening to go into the attic space. He immediately called 911, and the fire department came and put the fire out. Without Les getting awakened by his pet, the damage to the building, and perhaps worse, would have been extensive. As it happened, the damage was limited to the one unit, and it was minimal.

Chapter 9

Surviving the Great Recession

Like all entrepreneurs who launch a new business, survival becomes a way of life. This becomes apparent in the early stages of one's business startup. The survival techniques we used in the early years of our business and the lessons we learned enabled us to know how to make it through the great recession.

To be successful, every new business must overcome obstacles. The ability to problem solve with confidence in challenging situations is one of the keys to success in business as well as in life. Our philosophy has been that difficulties force us to be more resourceful, smarter, and more tenacious.

From the beginning, we had three problems: very little money, a lack of knowledge of the rental business, and no knowledge of construction. As students and teachers, we knew that we did not have to have all the answers—we just needed to know where to find them. Answers could be found by studying books, taking courses, and learning from others.

Our first problem was the shortage of money. When we started our business, we looked for sellers of existing apartments who would carry the mortgage for us or finance a second mortgage. As we began to build multifamily dwellings, we faced the large obstacle of convincing lending institutions to take a chance on two college music teachers who desired to build a real estate rental business.

For our first large project (108 units), we worked diligently to create the most convincing proposal that our study and efforts could produce. Carol, having completed a doctoral level course on writing proposals, created a beautiful one for our loan application. Although bankers were generally complimentary of our proposal, it was the *seventh* institution we approached that agreed to take a chance on us. Incidentally, since that early period, we have borrowed millions of dollars from the same bank that had such high praise for our proposal but could not help us at that time.

The second area of obstacles was our lack of knowledge of the construction process. With our first building project, a four-unit building, we began reading books on serving as one's own general contractor. The key ingredient was securing an experienced builder to aid and teach us since we were not only ignorant of building, but we were still full-time teachers and church musicians. In addition, our motto of the Golden Rule helped us to establish ongoing, mutually beneficial relationships with area subcontractors and professionals who became an integral part of our success.

The last area of weakness was our lack of knowledge of rental management. Starting small, with ten units and three houses, we read, studied, and learned as we grew. Perseverance and a desire to succeed were the keys to success. My philosophy was that we should be thankful for the difficulties inherent in rental real estate. If it were easy, everyone would do it, and it might not be as profitable.

Surviving became a way of life early in our business, but the great recession provided our company with the opportunity to refine and make all of our systems related to the management of our apartment communities better. Beginning in the fall of 2008, like other businesses, we have been challenged with the current economic climate. This downturn in the economy made it impossible to grow our business through development and construction, though we finished Hawthorn Suites, Orchard Park, Coryell Courts, and The Abbey.

We concentrated on refining and improving our existing properties and operation, and expanding the network to include third party owners. We currently manage 396 units for owners other than our family. We established our own brokerage, TLC Property Realty, in order to accommodate these third-party properties.

Under the leadership of our son, Sam, the company focused on efficiency, with a goal of reducing operating expenses by 10%. Fond of saying, "You can't control anything you don't measure," Sam began an analysis of current costs. The company saved $50,000 for fiscal 2009 by reorganizing and more closely measuring the fuel and insurance reimbursement program. For example, we found out that one of our service technicians was using a company vehicle *and* getting a monthly gas allowance. To add insult to injury, it was later determined that the service tech was getting the gas allowance every paycheck, which is every two weeks, instead of every month.

The first thing Sam did was standardize our books. Each property had its own bookkeeper, and each bookkeeper had their own chart of accounts. There was no way to take advantage of our large portfolio without first standardizing them. Therefore, we formalized a chart of accounts and began training all the bookkeepers on what goes into which account.

Next, we had to break each category into uniform units of measure. This was accomplished by measuring each cost category by month and per unit. For example, the "Repairs and Maintenance" category for Sherwood Village might be $60 per unit per month in a particular July. This system allowed us to compare the performance of one property with another and determine optimal operation ranges.

By consolidating our purchasing power, we were able to achieve an economy of scale. Instead of each property having accounts all over town, which is hard to control and measure, we purchased larger quantities of goods and services and received a better price. The savings were then passed on to the properties through the management company. This provided for thousands of dollars in savings.

Further analysis determined, which properties operated most efficiently in various areas, and those policies were established at every property. In short, we concentrated on effectiveness and belt-tightening.

TLC Properties is convinced that the company can weather the great recession without sacrificing our product, our service, or our reward system for our employee associates. By the grace of God, it is a time for us to be thankful for problems that challenge us toward new creativity and growth.

Due in large part to the "can do" attitude that we took as a company, we not only survived, but expanded our management company during the great recession. After all, it is during the tough times that we grow. This adage applies to businesses, as well as people. I would not like to go through the past four years again, but I am grateful for all that we learned as a company during that time.

FAQ: How Much Money Does One Need to Become Financially Independent?

When J. Paul Getty was asked this question late in his life, he said, "a little more." He also is given credit for saying that compound interest is the eighth wonder of the world. In real estate, how much you want to have or make is a matter of how many units you want to own. That question usually boils down to deciding how many units you want to manage.

At a business seminar on wealth accumulation that I attended in Santa Barbara, California, in 1985, the speaker said that the goal for each of us as we near retirement should be $1,000,000 in net worth that is somewhat liquid. He went on to say that only 7% of people reaching retirement age are in that category. The others are either broke or dead.

To accumulate $1,000,000 in net worth in real estate that is leveraged at 80% of its value, one would need to own $5,000,000 worth of real estate. This would include your home, as well as your rental holdings. Also, remember that if one has $1,000,000 of real estate debt, when that debt is paid off and the properties are free and clear, the owner is a millionaire.

Chapter 10

Leadership in Business

Leadership may be defined as the capacity to translate vision into reality. As a music teacher and minister for 30 years and a businessman and developer for the past 25 years, I have found this to be true in my development as a leader and in assisting others to develop their own leadership skills.

Leadership in the field of music demands a solid education background, including degrees and private study, to be the best teacher/performer that one can be. A successful music teacher/minister must see the potential in his students and clearly have the vision for them, and gently, but consistently, assist them to go beyond what they imagined. Leading others to become all that they can be requires:

- A keen desire to learn and develop
- A willingness to work hard
- A strong belief in one's ultimate success
- A love for people

The writer George Bernard Shaw once said, "Some people look at how things are and ask 'why,' while others dream of how things could be and ask 'why not.'" In the founding of TLC Properties, we looked ahead five to ten years, envisioned what apartment living would encompass at that time, and designed our product accordingly.

Sensing that women were the prime decision-makers in choosing apartments, we geared the floor plans to them—two baths in two-bedroom units, large closets, spacious baths, and appealing and modern kitchens.

Another important area of focus was the amenities. In addition to offering pools and recreation areas, we wanted our communities to have a resort feel. We included fitness centers, tanning beds, hot tubs, tot yards, movie theaters, and coffee and smoothie bars at some of our sites. Many of our communities include tennis and basketball courts, volleyball courts, and at one location, a putting green.

As professional musicians, Carol and I brought a strong aesthetic sensitivity to the business. Appealing architectural styles provide powerful curb appeal, and decorator quality interior design has resulted in apartments with a great single-family feel. We also established a reputation as an innovator in service.

TLC Properties has been a leader in making cable and Internet available at our cost to all residents, including it in their monthly rent from the very beginning. We have raised the standard in apartment dwellings and service. It is our desire to create an even better product and provide better service in the coming years. Our duty to our customers includes living up to our motto, the Golden Rule. We want to continue to treat our residents like we would want to be treated if we were the renter and they were the landlords. Our pledge is to continue to add meaning to our slogan, "We Are Apartments."

We feel that the discipline, organizational skills, perseverance, and aesthetic sensitivity gained in our educational pursuits and careers have contributed greatly to our success in our business. Our sons, Samuel, David, and Daniel, have all played vital roles in the development of our company. This successful family business is my proudest accomplishment to date.

Influencing the Success of Others

As college professors, our jobs were to prepare students for success by imparting knowledge and skill, encouraging diligence, high aspirations, and self-confidence. As a teacher, I had many opportunities to model, as well as instruct, since my work included both individual and class instruction. Most important to us was to engender a hunger for lifelong learning and growth.

As business leaders, we used all the skills that we had acquired in nurturing and developing the best in others in the music field. We have tried to use these skills and talents not only with our family members but also with our extended family, our friends, and employees.

We have considered our over-arching task to paint the big picture and provide the vision for the development of TLC Properties through the continued growth of our employees. As we communicated that vision and developed the means to translate it into reality, the company grew geometrically. With over eighty employees, we estimate that we employed an additional 3,000 contract workers over the past few years through the construction of some 2,500 units. Through our company, we have been blessed to assist dozens of family members and subcontractors in becoming financially independent.

Giving Back to Our Community

We have seen the importance of giving back to our community. One good way to do so is to get involved in civic affairs. Our desire is to thank Springfield for the blessings and opportunities that she has afforded us and also the belief that to whom much is given, much is required. It is a responsibility and privilege to participate in the law of reciprocity: If you give, it will be given to you.

TLC Properties has consistently supported local organizations, such as the March of Dimes. We also support groups like the Springfield Symphony Orchestra and the Springfield Regional Opera. Academic institutions, such as Evangel University and the James River Leadership College, have benefitted from the success of TLC Properties. Various members of our family have served on boards of directors in our city. We have long supported the Springfield Chamber of Commerce, and our company was chosen by the Chamber as the Best Small Business of the Year in 2009.

We strongly believe in giving back to the community in which one has prospered. We continue to look for ways that we can contribute to our church and community.

Give, and it will be given to you. A good measure, pressed down, shaken together and running over, will be poured into your lap. For with the measure you use, it will be measured to you (Lk. 6:38).

APPENDIX A

TLC Property Management

VISION:

Undisputed leadership in residential property management in the Midwest.

MISSION STATEMENT:

TLC Property Management is a biblically based company that provides premier properties and superb service, rewarding and challenging employment, and maximum profits to property owners. We are passionately committed to excellence and integrity.

SLOGAN: *WE ARE APARTMENTS*

MOTTO: Do unto others as you would have them do unto you (Mt. 7:12).

PLEDGE TO RESIDENTS: Our residents are our friends. Without you, we would not have a job. Therefore, we strive to be:

- Courteous
- Friendly
- Fair
- Attentive
- Prompt

PLEDGE TO EMPLOYEES

TLC Property Management will:

- Train you thoroughly
- Treat you fairly
- Deal with you kindly
- Reward you generously

ROLE OF SUPERVISORS

It is our job:

- To hold those we supervise accountable for their responsibilities
- To serve them—servant leadership

PLEDGE TO PROPERTY OWNERS

TLC Property Management will strive to:

- Maximize your profits with superior management and customer service
- Increase the value of your investment
- Represent and work for you as diligently as we do our own properties

APPENDIX B

Passing the Torch: January 2009 (Speech delivered to the TLC Properties staff at our bi-weekly luncheon)

As you may have heard by now, Carol and I have decided to take a step back from the day-to-day operation of TLC Properties. We will still be around. In fact, I still plan on visiting you at your communities and at the job sites. We will also retain our titles of President and CEO, respectively.

The torch has been passed on to a new generation. The vision that God gave to Carol and me is nearing completion, and we proudly hand off the baton to our sons. Sam Jr. will be most responsible for the daily activities. God has given him a vision for fantastic and exciting expansion of TLC Properties—a vision with which I completely concur.

At this juncture of my life, I can't help but think of my parents, Morrison and Oma Coryell. My dad was a self-employed tailor who raised seven children, earning, in a good year, about a $100 per week. He taught us to be frugal. Turn off the lights, preserve water, eat everything on your plate—all were admonitions that I took to heart. Sam Jr. said once that if I ever had an out-of-body experience and saw the light at the end of the tunnel, I would ask someone to "turn off that light."

I learned my lessons well. However, probably the most important lesson my father instilled in me, other than his faith, was an intense desire and, indeed, a passion for education. I knew that my avenue to whatever God had for me involved getting as much education as I could get. By the time I was in junior high school, I knew that somehow, someway, I would go to college.

With my father's help, and a little help from Uncle Sam, I not only went to college but was able to obtain three degrees from three outstanding universities. It was through our education that we ended up in Springfield, teaching at Evangel University.

I won't bore you with the details of how this business got started and grew, because many of you heard much of that story last year at our January banquet. I'll simply say that God did, indeed, give me a vision—one that I knew would take the rest of my professional life to achieve.

We leave TLC Properties in strong and capable hands. Sam Jr. came to work for me thirteen years ago this month [January 2009]. Dan and Dave followed a couple of years later. Sam has been my right arm. I truly can't remember the last time we had a serious disagreement. I know that I love and trust him, and I feel that you will love and trust him as you work with him and get to know him.

Sam, like Solomon of old, you asked God for wisdom, and in my opinion, He answered your prayer. I happily pass the baton to you. May God richly bless you as you lead TLC Properties. May you realize your vision as fully and completely as God enabled me to realize mine.

—*Dr. Sam Coryell*

About the Author

Dr. Sam Coryell has had two successful careers—one in music at Evangel University and the second one in real estate development in Springfield, Missouri. Sam and his wife, Carol, raised three sons who have, in turn, participated closely in the real estate business.

Sam's specialty in real estate was in developing multifamily apartment complexes to meet the needs of the community. A tribute to his expert design and concern for his tenants is that many of his complexes were almost entirely rented by the time they initially opened.

Sam can often be found at the forefront of giving back not only in his church, but in many community efforts, sponsoring various events for charities.

To contact Sam to book speaking engagements or to obtain bulk orders of books, write or call:

TLC Properties
1531 E. Bradford Pkwy., Suite 305
Springfield MO 65804
(417) 869-1118